Home Closing Checklist

Other McGraw-Hill Books by Robert Irwin

Home Closing Checklist

Robert Irwin

McGraw-Hill

New York   Chicago   San Francisco   Lisbon   London   Madrid   Mexico City
Milan   New Delhi   San Juan   Seoul   Singapore   Sydney   Toronto

This publication is designed to provide accurate and authoritative information in regard to the subject matter covered. It is sold with the understanding that neither the author nor the publisher is engaged in rendering legal, accounting, futures/securities trading, real estate, or other professional service. If legal advice or other expert assistance is required, the services of a competent professional person should be sought.

—From a Declaration of Principles jointly adopted by a Committee of the American Bar Association and a Committee of Publishers

McGraw-Hill books are available at special quantity discounts to use as premiums and sales promotions, or for use in corporate training programs. For more information, please write to the Director of Special Sales, Professional Publishing, McGraw-Hill, Two Penn Plaza, New York, NY 10121-2298. Or contact your local bookstore.

 This book is printed on recycled, acid-free paper containing a minimum of 50% recycled, de-inked fiber.

Library of Congress Cataloging-in-Publication Data

Irwin, Robert.
   Home closing checklist / by Robert Irwin.
      p. cm.
   ISBN 0-07-140997-1 (alk. paper)
1. House buying—United States.   2. Settlement costs—United States.
3. Residential real estate—United States—Finance.   4. Mortgage loans—United States.   I. Title.
 HD259.I783 2004
   643'.12—dc22

2003014816

Contents

Part 2 Closing the Offer

5. Negotiating the Closing Costs   63

6. Creating a Powerful Purchase Agreement   71

Questions to Ask My Agent

Questions to Ask the Home Inspector (When You Go Along)

Part 4   Closing the Escrow

10. Finding a Reliable Escrow–Title Insurance Company   **139**

Questions to Ask Yourself

Questions to Ask the Escrow–Title Insurance Company

11. Removing Contingencies   **145**

Questions You Should Ask Yourself

Questions to Ask Your Escrow Holder or Agent

Introduction

Steps to Closing a Real Estate Transaction

Everyone knows when a real estate deal closes: It's when you get the keys to the house and the sellers get their money. But when does the closing process actually begin?

In truth, it starts when you make an offer to purchase. How that offer is written up determines what steps you have to take in order to eventually receive possession of your new home.

There are many steps involved in the closing. These can include getting financing, clearing contingencies and title, and paying closing costs (see the list that follows). There also can be many stumbling blocks. For example, your lender or escrow company may charge excessive garbage fees or may refuse to fund, or the escrow holder may make mistakes, or clouds (defects) may appear on the title.

Or it could go quickly and smoothly.

In this book we'll cover all aspects of closing a transaction from having the purchase agreement written up correctly to determining which closing costs are fair and which ones are nothing more than "garbage." We'll see your options in avoiding garbage fees, we'll do the final walk-through, and we'll explain all about lenders. We'll do it in the form of a checklist that will explain what questions you should ask, whom you should ask, and what answers you should expect.

To get started, it's important that you have a sense of what's involved in a typical residential real estate closing. So here it is, step by step:

Ten Steps to Closing a Home Purchase

1. Present a written offer to the seller.
2. Have the seller accept and sign your offer.
3. Open an escrow account, negotiate the escrow and title costs, and sign the preliminary instructions.
4. Secure financing, and negotiate lender closing costs. (You should already be preapproved for financing.)
5. Read and approve the seller's disclosures.
6. Obtain and approve a professional property inspection, and approve other reports as needed.
7. Check the title and remove contingencies from your offer.
8. Complete any remaining escrow work, and do the final walk-through.
9. Get funded by your lender.
10. Sign the final escrow instructions (also called *closing the escrow*), and pay your remaining down payment and closing costs.

None of it is hard to do, and all of it is covered in the following chapters. If you do it correctly, you'll soon be receiving the key to your new home. And you'll be able to tell everyone what a terrific deal you got!

1

Understanding the Closing and Its Costs

1
What Are Closing Costs?

QUESTIONS TO ASK YOURSELF

What are closing costs?

☐

Closing costs are transaction costs—charges in addition to the amount that you pay for a property. They are charges on top of the purchase price. For example, if you buy a home for $250,000, your purchase price typically will consist of your down payment and your new mortgage. However, added to this will be an additional amount for closing costs. Closing costs typically run 3 to 7 percent of the purchase price for the buyer, 7 to 10 percent for the seller. (Both buyer and seller have their own, separate closing costs.) Closing costs are normally paid in cash, so it's important that you have enough money to cover both your down payment *and* your closing costs.

Are closing costs fair and reasonable?

☐

Some are, and some aren't. A few closing costs are regulated by the government, and by and large, most lenders and others who set closing costs charge fair and reasonable fees. One serious problem, however, has been *garbage fees*, charges that are either higher than actual costs or charges that you, the buyer, should not have to pay. A second serious problem with some lenders has been *lowballing*, where actual costs at closing have been higher by up to thousands of dollars than estimates given at the time you applied for the mortgage.

Who will tell me what my closing costs are for the purchase I am presently making?

It is difficult to know exactly what your closing costs will be until the close of escrow. However, when you make your offer, a good real estate agent should be able to give you a fairly accurate estimate. (Some very good agents can come within $50 of actual costs!) When you apply for a mortgage, your lender will also give you a Real Estate Settlement Procedures Act (RESPA) fair estimate of your potential costs. However, in too many cases estimates have been off by as much as thousands of dollars, causing buyer-borrowers not to rely on them. Your title insurance-escrow company will also give you an estimate of your costs at the time you open escrow. However, again, these estimates may be wildly off. At least 1 day before the deal closes, you'll be given a HUD-1 form that details exactly what all of your closing costs are. Of course, by then, it's usually too late to do anything about them.

Why do I have to pay closing costs?

Buying a house is unlike most other transactions. When you buy furniture or even a car, you are usually dealing only with the seller. Therefore, all the money you pay goes directly to the seller. (With a car, you do have some closing costs such as registration and license fees that you pay to the government.) When you buy a home, however, while some of your purchase price does usually go to the seller, there are many other parties who contribute to making the deal. And in order to get their services, they must be paid. They include the following:

- Lender(s)
- Title company
- Escrow company
- Attorney
- Real estate agent
- Home inspector
- Termite/pest inspector

- Appraiser
- Others

Each of these other "entities" may contribute something to making your deal possible. And because of that, they demand, and are entitled to, a fee. Their fees represent your closing costs.

Can I get out of paying closing costs?

Not usually, but sometimes. There are really only two ways to get out of paying closing costs. The first is to negotiate them down with whoever is charging them. It may be possible to have them reduced, or sometimes eliminated. The other alternative is to have someone else pay your closing costs for you. Sometimes a builder, for example, will pay a buyer's closing costs in order to induce that buyer to make a purchase. In other cases, a seller may be willing to pay your closing costs. *Note:* Do not confuse having your closing costs financed (added into the mortgage) with not paying them. When they are financed, you may not put out the cash at the closing, but you will pay for the costs over the course of the loan (see below).

Can the seller pay my closing costs?

In theory almost anyone can pay your closing costs for you. However, the most likely person to do this is the seller. When you negotiate for the purchase of the property, you can bargain not only for price and terms but for closing costs as well. In a buyer's market, where there are many properties for sale and few takers, sellers will often agree to pay at least a portion of the buyer's closing costs in order to make the sale. This is particularly helpful to many cash-strapped buyers because it means they need to put less cash into the transaction. (In a seller's market the seller may want you, the buyer, to pay his or her closing costs!)

What are *recurring* and *nonrecurring* closing costs?

Closing costs that recur are such things as interest on your mortgage, taxes, and insurance payments. They are ongoing, payable monthly or annually. Nonrecurring closing costs (NRCC) are one-time charges. These include points on your mortgage (discussed in Chapter 2), title insurance, and escrow fees.

Will lenders allow the seller to pay my closing costs?

Lenders can be strict about not allowing the seller to pay all your costs. Usually they will allow it if the costs are nonrecurring or one-time only charges. On the other hand, they may refuse to give you a needed mortgage if the seller is paying your recurring costs. The thinking here is that if you can't handle recurring costs, you probably can't afford to take out the mortgage.

Will having someone else pay my closing costs affect my taxes?

Someone else's paying your closing costs shouldn't have an effect on your annual property taxes, but it could have an effect on your income taxes. Usually mortgage interest and some points (usually those charged to obtain a new mortgage) are deductible from your federal and state income taxes. However, this may not be the case if someone else pays them for you. You should check with your accountant before negotiating for the seller to pay your closing costs to see what the tax consequences for you will be.

Do I have to pay the lender's closing costs?

Usually. Lenders' closing costs have been rising and may include some of the most irritating garbage fees (described in the next several chapters). Further, a few lenders have become notorious for initially underestimating the true closing costs they will charge you. On the other hand, it is possible to get *no-fee loans*. Here, there are no closing costs at all immediately charged to you—you instead "finance" them. The catch is that in order to get a no-fee mortgage, you will either have to pay a higher interest rate or you will have to have the fees added to your mortgage amount. The most common practice, charging a higher-than-market interest rate, usually means you'll pay about three-eighths of 1 percent more for your loan. But it may be worth it to you to not have to come up with the cash for closing costs. (See also Chapter 2.)

Do I have to pay closing costs to my agent?

Sometimes. Usually the seller pays the commission for selling the home (typically 6 percent). However, in a seller's market where there is a very low inventory of homes and plentiful buyers, sometimes as a condition of sale, the seller may insist you pay a portion of this charge. Further, if you use a buyer's agent, you may be on the hook for this buyer's agent's commission, although buyers' agents are usually very good at getting their fee out of the commission the sellers pay. Finally, you may be asked to pay a *transaction fee* (or something similarly named), which is an additional amount of money, typically around $500, which goes to the real estate agent's company for handling the transaction. Transaction fees are a fairly recent new charge, and many buyers hotly contest paying them. (See also Chapter 13.)

Do I have to pay closing costs to an attorney?

If you are in parts of the East Coast, chances are you have an attorney handling the closing of your home purchase. Typically attorneys in this part of the country charge between $500 and $1500 for handling all of the closing work. You will be asked to pay this fee by your attorney. However, you may not be required to pay an additional escrow fee, and your title insurance fee could be lower. In addition, you may be asked to pay other attorneys. For example, your lender may ask you to pay its attorney for putting the loan documents together. This is usually considered a garbage fee since the lender should be paying its own attorney's fees. Be sure to question why you are paying any attorney's fees other than those of your own lawyer.

Do I have to pay closing costs to a title insurance company?

The matter of who pays for title insurance, the buyer or the seller, is a matter of custom. In many areas the buyer pays. In other areas it's the seller. And in some parts of the country, the fee is split. Keep in mind that you are not required to obtain title insurance. However, a lender will always require it. And even if you pay cash and do not use a lender, you should still get this insurance. It protects you in case there is a problem with the title to the property, which can happen in real estate. For example, it might be discovered sometime in the future that the seller had an undisclosed partner on the deed, and that partner may want a money settlement. In that case, the title insurance will cover your loss up to the amount of your insurance (which is usually the amount of the purchase price). If you are obtaining financing to make the purchase, the lender will usually insist that the amount of the mortgage be fully covered by a *lender's policy of title insurance*, which you also will have to pay for.

Do I have to pay closing costs to the escrow company?

It is important to understand that the escrow is different from title insurance. The escrow holder is a stakeholder, typically an independent and licensed company (or possibly an attorney) who gathers all the documents needed to close the transaction (such as the seller's deed to you) and all monies and then, when everything is "perfect," records the deed and pays out the money to the sellers and other parties. For this function the escrow holder demands a fee. Who pays the fee, depends on local custom, just as it does for title insurance. In some areas the seller pays the entire amount. In other areas it's the buyer. In most parts of the country the fee is split down the middle with buyer and seller each paying half. Sometimes there are additional garbage fees charged by the escrow holder.

Do I have to pay closing costs to the state and/or federal government?

There are usually some fees to be paid. For example, most states charge a *transfer tax*, which is usually a nominal amount. Either the buyer or seller will be required to pay this fee. At this time there is no federal sales tax on homes; however, this is something that Congress has toyed with at different times. You will also usually have to pay a portion of your state and/or local property taxes. This amount is typically *prorated*, which means that since the tax is paid once or twice annually, you'll pay just your share for the time you will own the property, and the sellers will pay theirs for the time the property was in their names.

Can I get my closing costs paid back if I resell soon?

Sometimes. For example, if you get an FHA mortgage as part of your purchase and then, within a year or two, sell the property and pay off that loan, a significant amount of the mortgage insurance fee (which you paid up front as a closing cost) can be redeemed by contacting the FHA. In addition, the escrow company will usually get an extra few hundred dollars from you to cover unforeseen closing costs. When these don't materialize, you may receive a check back for this amount within a month after the purchase. Finally, if you resell within around a year, you may be able to negotiate a reissue fee for the title insurance, escrow charges, and loan fees if you use the same companies on your next home purchase.

Are there new government protections available to me?

The U.S. Department of Housing and Urban Development (HUD) has come up with a system that it hopes will help curb abuses (not yet implemented as of this writing). When you apply for a mortgage, your lender will be required to give you two options. The first is essentially what we have now, which is offering you a *fair estimate* of what your closing costs will be. It's called a *good-faith estimate (GFE)*. However, the lender does not guarantee these costs will remain the same at closing—they could be higher. The second option is to guarantee that your closing costs will not be higher than those quoted when you applied for your loan. This option is called the *guaranteed-mortgage package agreement* (GMPA). Here, the fees would, presumably, be guaranteed to be exactly the same at closing as they were quoted when you applied for the mortgage. However, for this guaranteed service, the lender can charge higher fees as well as a higher interest rate. Thus, when applying for a loan, you can shop for lenders to find the one that offers you the best package at the lowest cost. However, in reality you the consumer are left once again holding the bag. The reason is that in most cases, lenders can come surprisingly close to estimating

actual closing costs. Thus, if you choose the pricier guaranteed closing costs, you will be paying extra for a service
that the lender can perform, in most cases, without extra
cost to it. On the other hand, if you choose the less costly
estimated service, lenders may feel perfectly justified in
hiking costs at closing. Keep in mind that this two-tiered
structure has not been implemented as of this writing.

2
Lenders' Closing Costs

GENERAL QUESTIONS YOU SHOULD ASK

What are *loan closing fees*?

These are fees that a lender charges you when you obtain a mortgage. Many of the fees represent the actual costs of preparing and funding the loan. For example, to get financing, in most cases you will need to get an appraisal of the home you are buying. An appraiser is sent out who determines the property's market value. Typically the cost is around $350. This is a lender's closing fee that you will probably be asked to pay at the time the deal closes (see Chapter 1 for an explanation of the closing procedure). Another common lender's fee is for a credit report that the lender uses to determine if you are a qualified buyer. Some lenders charge you for this report, while others absorb the cost themselves. There are many other lenders' closing fees. Some are reasonable, and some are what many people consider unwarranted, or garbage. To get the mortgage, however, you must pay the fees or negotiate with the lender to lower them or eliminate them.

Why do lenders charge closing fees?

Some lenders' closing fees are actual expenses the lender incurred in writing the loan, such as the property appraisal fee, and the lender is just passing those costs along to you. In other cases, however, the lender is using these fees to legitimately increase its yield (return) on the mortgage. This is accomplished by giving you less money than you actually want to borrow. For example, if you are borrowing $100,000 on a 6 percent interest rate mortgage (30 years), the lender may discount the loan by $2500 (or 2.5 points). Thus, the amount of money actually advanced to you by the lender will be only $97,500. Since you need the full $100,000 to complete the purchase, you'll have to come up with the remaining $2500 out of your pocket. From the lender's perspective, however, having you pay 6 percent interest on a $100,000 loan while giving you only $97,500 results in an actual increase in yield to about 6.25 percent. The yield to the lender is higher than the interest rate charged to you because less money is advanced, which is a big reason that lenders discount mortgages and charge loan closing fees.

Do I have to pay closing fees?

It really depends on how savvy a borrower you are. If you get a "no-fee" or "guaranteed-fee" mortgage with a lender or negotiate out of any closing fees (*at the time you apply!*), then you probably won't be asked to pay any. On the other hand, if you wait until the deal is ready to close and then decide to complain about fees, you probably will still have to pay them or lose the loan and the deal and anger the seller.

What are *garbage fees*?

These are closing costs to you from some lenders that either are not actual expenses or, if they are actual expenses, are those that the lender should pay, not you. They can sometimes be quite substantial, in some cases mounting up into the thousands of dollars. Borrower-buyer complaints about these fees have been widespread, and they have gotten the nickname "garbage fees." They have been the subject of scrutiny by HUD, which in 2003 released new rules for closings. However, as of this writing these new closing procedures have not been adopted. Reasonable people can disagree over which fees are garbage and which are legitimate. In the subsequent questions and answers, I give you my interpretation.

Who determines which fees are reasonable and which are garbage?

There is no set arbiter of fees. Any fee that a lender charges might be a reasonable cost, or it might simply be a garbage fee. It all depends on what services you've asked the lender for and which it is actually performing for you. That, of course, is what makes it all so confusing to buyer-borrowers. *Note:* It is important to understand that not all lenders charge garbage fees. Indeed, most lenders' fees are quite legitimate.

Why do some lenders charge garbage fees?

These fees are another way that some lenders can increase their yield (profit) while sometimes confusing the borrower into thinking he or she is actually paying less. It works like this: Like the discount noted above, garbage fees reduce the amount of money that the lender actually provides to you. If, for example, there are $2500 of garbage fees on a 6 percent interest rate mortgage of $100,000 (30 years), plus the $2500 discount noted above (total $5000), the lender will advance you only $95,000. You'll owe $100,000, but you'll only get $95,000, meaning you must come up with $5000 in additional closing costs out of your pocket. However, the lender who advances only $95,000 on a 6 percent interest rate, $100,000 mortgage actually gets a yield of approximately 6.5 percent. The garbage fees increase the lender's yield, thus earning it more money. Since few borrowers actually understand this process, a few unscrupulous lenders will advertise a lower 6 percent interest rate, attracting unsuspecting borrowers, then tack on both the discount *and* the garbage fees, boosting the true yield to 6.5 percent. A scrupulous lender, on the other hand, would be up front about it and simply say the interest rate was discounted 6.25 percent and then charge no garbage fees.

Do lenders mark up their costs?

Some do. For example, a three-bureau credit report (from all three national credit reporting agencies) may cost a lender $20. Yet, the lender might charge you $60 for that report. Or it might charge you only $20. This is an area that is presently in flux. HUD has said that markups *without* a third party involved (a third party means that someone else obtained the credit report, marked it up, and then sold it to the lender who simply passed the markup along to you) generally should *not* be permitted. However, litigation brought in several states by various real estate interests has upheld the right to mark up costs. As a result, some of the costs that you see on your closing statement such as credit report, courier, mailing, and other fees may have been marked up.

Can I switch lenders if I don't like the fees?

You can always switch lenders; however, the problems that can occur by doing so, particularly at the time of closing, may be so large that you will not want to do it. For example, if you paid an advance fee to get your loan, you might lose that money if you later switch lenders. Even more significant, you signed a purchase agreement that almost certainly had strict deadlines. At the close of escrow you have very little time left, almost certainly not enough to get a new lender. Hence, switching then could cause you to lose the deal. Not only could that result in your not getting the home but also in your losing your deposit. And an angry seller could potentially even sue you! The time to switch lenders is when you're first looking for one, when you have time on your side, not when the deal is ready to close.

Can I get a mortgage without closing costs?

Yes, and no. Today no-fee mortgages are readily available. When you get these, the lender will not charge you any fees—no discount, no garbage fees, no costs of any kind. However, the costs are still there. Instead of paying them as closing costs, they are built into the mortgage in one of two ways—either by increasing the mortgage amount or by increasing the interest rate (typically by around three-eights of 1 percent). The advantage is that you don't need to take money out of your pocket to pay loan closing costs. (Sometimes these mortgages will pay *all* your closing costs including title insurance!) Of course, you'll end up with either a bigger loan or a higher interest rate and resulting higher monthly payments. (See Chapter 9 for more information on these types of loans.)

SPECIFIC FEES YOU SHOULD UNDERSTAND (ALPHABETICALLY)

What are *numbered fees*?

These are specifically named charges that HUD lists in its HUD-1 settlement worksheet that must be presented to you at least 1 day prior to closing. The common closing fees are specified here. However, many new or creative fees also can be listed in this document as well. Explanations for the following fees (plus other more creative ones) are given in the following questions and answers in this chapter.

Designated Fees on the HUD-1 Statement

700. Broker's commission

801. Loan origination fee

802. Loan discount

803. Appraisal fee

804. Credit report fee

805. Lender's inspection fee

806. Mortgage insurance application fee

807. Assumption fee

808–811. Left blank

901. Interest

902. Mortgage insurance premium

903. Hazard insurance premium

904–905. Left blank

1001. Hazard insurance reserve

1002. Mortgage insurance reserve

1003. City property tax reserve

1004. County property tax reserve

1005. Annual assessments

1101. Settlement or closing fee

1102. Abstract or title search fee

1103. Title examination fee

1104. Title insurance binder

1105. Document preparation fee

1106. Notary fees

1107. Attorney's fees

1108. Title insurance premium

1109. Lender's coverage

1110. Owner's coverage

1201. Recording fees

1202. City and/or county tax stamps

1203. State tax stamps

1301. Survey fee

1302. Pest inspection fee

1303–1305. Left blank for additional settlement charges

What is an *administrative fee?*

This usually refers to the lender's underwriting and processing costs. However, be sure that the lender isn't additionally charging separately for those costs. For example, if you have an administration fee and then also fees for underwriting, document preparation, and other items, it's questionable. Also, be sure that the administration fee is comparable to what other lenders charge for a similar service. *Note:* To some lenders an administration fee is the difference between the market rate for the loan and a premium they are paying if your loan is below market. Be careful, here, since this could be a clandestine form of discounting or increasing the loan's yield to them.

What is an *appraisal fee?*

This charge covers the lender's expense for having the property you are buying evaluated to determine its market value. No lender will normally give you a mortgage without such an appraisal. It usually involves having the appraiser actually go out to the property and walk through it as well as compare it to recent sales of similar homes. (Sometimes quicker appraisals, referred to as *drive-bys,* are made, and for these the inspector never really goes into the house.) More recently, a national database of property values from across the country has been established, and if the home you are considering was sold in the previous 5 years or so, it may already be in this database. In that case the lender may not actually need a formal appraisal but may instead simply check the database to determine the market value of the house. In either case, however, the lender may charge you a fee. The typical fee today is around $250 to $350. This is a normal and necessary lender's closing fee for a formal, physical appraisal, and it is a fee that you should expect to pay. The fee should be less for a drive-by or a database check.

What is an *assumption fee?*

Although it is rarely done these days, it is possible to assume an existing loan from a seller. Most FHA and Veterans' Administration (VA) loans in the past were fully assumable (no qualifying). Many adjustable-rate mortgages (ARMs) and current FHA and VA loans are likewise assumable today but with qualifying. In fact, in order to assume most mortgages, today's lenders require that the buyer be qualified almost as stringently as if he or she were obtaining a brand-new loan. And often the lenders will raise the interest rate to current market levels. If you are assuming a loan, the lender may also impose an assumption fee to cover its costs in transferring the existing loan to your name. This fee can be small, only a few hundred dollars, or it could be much more depending on the lender. Assumption fees have been around for decades, and as long as they aren't unreasonably high, they are considered a normal part of assuming an existing loan. You should get information on what your assumption fee will be at the time you apply for the assumption.

What is a *buydown fee?*

It is possible to get the interest rate on a mortgage reduced by paying a fee directly to the lender—the higher the fee, the lower the interest rate. When you are obtaining the mortgage yourself, this is commonly called a *discount*. When someone else is doing it for you (or you for someone else), it's called a *buydown*. For example, a builder may buy down the interest rate on a mortgage in order to get you, the buyer, a lower interest rate (and, hence, payment) so you will be more inclined to purchase a home. The buydown fee may show up as part of the closing statement, even though it's a fee you probably aren't going to be paying.

What is a *circumvention fee?*

Some mortgage brokers incorporate a clause into their loan applications that states that if you should decide not to go with this particular mortgage broker but instead obtain a loan, loan approval, loan commitment, or even make a loan application to a lender whom this mortgage broker has previously solicited on your behalf, you owe this broker a circumvention fee. The charge is imposed because, presumably, you tried to circumvent (go around) this mortgage broker and get the loan directly from the lender. Some sophisticated buyer-borrowers may attempt to circumvent the loan broker they originally worked with, presumably to avoid paying the mortgage broker's commission. If this fee appears on your closing statement, you may want to dispute it since the mortgage broker who is claiming it is not normally a part of the transaction: He or she is not the buyer, the seller, or the lender. This fee is usually a matter to be settled outside of escrow, between the loan broker who wants to collect it and yourself.

What is a *commitment fee?*

A commitment fee to a borrower is usually a charge the lender makes for committing to give you a mortgage. In exchange for being assured that upon closing the transaction you'll have the loan money you need at the terms agreed upon, you'll now pay a set amount of money, typically a few hundred dollars. It is similar to a *lock-in fee*, except that it's usually given only after you've completely qualified for the mortgage. In most transactions a loan commitment is given without a fee; hence, some people consider this type of fee to be a garbage charge.

What is a *county, city,* or *state tax stamp?*

Depending on where you live in the country, your city, county, or state may tax the transfer of your property.

Typically this is in the form of *stamps* (similar to postage stamps) that are purchased for so much per thousand dollars and then affixed to the deed. Usually these fees aren't very high, amounting to no more than a few hundred dollars for most residential transactions. Your escrow company should take care of buying these stamps for you. However, you can expect to find the costs of these stamps charged to you somewhere on your closing statement. If you are being charged just for the exact cost of the stamps, it's a normal and necessary part of the closing.

What is a *courier fee?*

In order to close an escrow within the optimal time frame, sometimes loan and other documents must be hand carried. Courier services are available in most metropolitan areas, and if your lender used such services, this fee covers the charge for them. You should ask yourself two questions: Is such extraordinary service really necessary? And is this just the courier fee, or has it been marked up? Unfortunately, it can be difficult to get straight answers to either question. One solution is to refuse to authorize any courier fees. However, by so doing you could jeopardize the loan you hope to get and also the deal itself. A courier charge, therefore, though sometimes a garbage fee and sometimes legitimate, is hard to argue with.

What is a *credit reporting fee?*

Before giving you a mortgage, your lender will want a credit report on your credit history, typically a report that takes into account all three national bureaus (TransUnion, Experion, and Equifax—see the Internet resources at the back of the book for Web addresses). Some lenders will simply absorb this fee under the name of good business. Others, however, will want you to pay the fee, and, hence, it could appear on your closing documents. If the lender wants you to pay it, you'll have to do that. However, the question that now arises is whether or not the lender marked up the cost of obtaining the report. Although sometimes these reports can be obtained for as little as $20, they can also cost more, as much as $50. You may want to challenge a credit reporting fee much higher than that.

What is a *discount*?

A discount means that you're not getting your loan at face value. Loans are discounted by *points* (see below). If you get a $100,000 mortgage with 5 points, the amount of money that will actually be forwarded to escrow for you will be only $95,000. The discount favors the lender, not you, and it is used to give the lender a higher yield than the stated interest rate. You can usually (not always) determine the true interest rate by checking the APR (annual percentage rate) on your loan documents, which normally includes the discount. Mortgage discounts came into heavy use in the 1950s when rising interest rates kept borrowers away from real estate. With discounts, lenders could seem to offer lower interest rates and thereby attract buyers back into the market. During periods of very low interest rates, as during the early 2000s, discounts virtually disappear. They are seen mostly during periods of high interest rates, as during the 1980s.

What is a *document preparation fee*?

To get a mortgage, you will need to sign a variety of documents possibly including a mortgage, trust deed, and note. Some of these documents may include IRS statements, equal housing opportunity disclosures, and others that may be relative to the state you are in. It is not uncommon to have upwards of 50 pages of documents to look over and initial or sign. While the preparation of these documents in today's world with computers typically requires no more than the press of a few keystrokes, someone must still decide which documents you need to sign and get them ready. Therefore, some lenders have begun charging you, the borrower, for their preparation. To my mind, this is strictly a garbage fee. The preparation of loan documents should be a cost of business assumed by a lender. You shouldn't have to pay for them anymore than you would pay for the preparation of a receipt you get when you buy a refrigerator.

What is an *escrow waiver fee*?

If you have an FHA, VA, or conventional loan for more than 80 percent of the property's value, you must have an escrow impound account that pays your taxes and insurance for you (and into which you pay one-twelfth of these costs each month). However, if you put down 80 percent or more of the property's value, you aren't required to have an escrow account. Recently, lenders have taken to charging a fee, called an escrow waiver fee, to those who don't want this escrow account. The fee can sometimes be substantial, in the form of a higher interest rate. To my way of thinking, this is just another junk fee. Seek out a lender who doesn't require the escrow waiver fee.

What is a *first-year flood insurance fee?*

Before a lender will give you a mortgage, it wants to have some assurance that the property is secure against water damage. After all, it's not a personal loan; it's a real estate loan. If the house is on a flood plain or is subject to flooding from nearby lakes, streams, or even the ocean, the lender will insist that you carry sufficient insurance to at least pay off the mortgage in the event your home is destroyed by flood. (It may require you carry enough insurance to cover rebuilding the home.) When you close escrow, to demonstrate that you, indeed, do have such flood insurance, you'll have to pay at least 1 year's premium. Unless you've paid for this insurance outside escrow, you can expect it to show up as a fee. While this is a normal part of getting financing, you are not required to get insurance with an insurance company affiliated with the lender. You should, in fact, shop around for the best, cheapest policy that you can find.

What is a *first-year hazard insurance fee?*

Similarly, before a lender will give you a mortgage, it wants to have some assurance that the property is secure against fire and other types of damage. After all, if the house burns down and you don't have insurance coverage, the party most likely to lose the most will be the lender. Therefore, it will insist that you carry sufficient insurance to at least pay off the mortgage in the event your home is destroyed by fire. (It may require you carry enough insurance to cover rebuilding the home.) When you close escrow, to demonstrate that you, indeed, do have such fire or hazard insurance, you'll normally have to pay at least 1 year's premium. Unless you've paid for this insurance outside escrow, you can expect it to show up as a fee. While this is a normal part of getting financing, you are not required to get insurance with an insurance company affiliated with the lender. You should, in fact, shop around for the best, cheapest policy that you can find.

What is a *flood certification fee?*

This is to pay for a certification that states your home's physical relationship to a flood plain or other similar flood area. Preparing this certificate requires that someone check out flood maps and locate your home on the maps to establish whether it's within or outside of certain flood plain boundaries. The fee for doing that work and issuing the certificate is often part of the closing fees.

What is a *funding fee?*

This is a fee that the lender may charge you for funding the money for your mortgage. The fee is imposed because there could be a short period of time between the date the money is forwarded to your escrow and the date the escrow actually closes during which the lender actually doesn't collect interest on it. Since the amounts involved are typically very large (a $200,000 or $300,000 mortgage is not uncommon), even short periods of time can be costly to the lender who funds early. On the other hand, with wire transfers being extremely common and relatively inexpensive, there's no real reason for the lender to fund the money until the actual moment the escrow is ready to close, unless the escrow officer errs in calling for funds too early. Therefore, there's no real reason that you should pay for the lender's inability to fund in a timely manner or the escrow officer's error.

What is a *home inspection fee?*

This can cover several possible charges. One is for the lender's inspector to go out to the property and check that it actually exists, that the boundaries are as stated, and so on. A minimal fee may be charged here, although this should be a normal-course-of-business expense for the lender. Also, today it is common practice to have a professional inspector take a look at your home before you buy it. There are two reasons for this: The first is to discover any defects that you might have missed yourself. And the second is to renegotiate the terms and price of the transaction in order to more closely reflect the true (as uncovered by the inspection) condition of the home. If you order the professional inspection, then it's up to you to pay for it. The charge is usually around $250 to $350 depending on the size of the home and the nature of the inspection. Most inspectors will want their money up front. That is, they will want to be paid on the spot at the completion of the inspection. Some will accept a check, but others will want cash. The reason is that they want to be sure to be paid, even if you subsequently decide not to go through with the purchase. On the other hand, sometimes an inspector will agree to be paid out of escrow. This is often the case when someone else orders the inspection for you, such as a real estate agent. If that's the case, a home inspection fee will appear on your closing statement. Unless it's an overcharge, it's a normal and usual fee.

What is an *impound setup fee?*

Whenever you get a mortgage for 80 percent or more of the value of the property, you will be required to carry two things: private mortgage insurance (PMI) and an impounded account. The PMI insures the lender in the event that you default on your payments. The impounded account is like an escrow account. Each month one-twelfth of your annual tax and insurance payment will be deposited to it from your monthly mortgage payment. [Your mortgage payment will be enlarged to cover principal, interest, taxes, and insurance (PITI).] The lender will impound this amount for you in your account, and when your taxes and insurance are due, it will pay them out of the account. (You can choose to not use an impounded account, at your option, if your mortgage is for less than 80 percent of property value.) Some lenders charge a fee for setting up the impounded account. If yours does, that fee will be reflected on the closing statement. To my way of thinking, this is, again, a necessary part of doing business for the lender, and you shouldn't be charged a fee. On the other hand, if it's less than $50, it's probably not worth arguing about.

What is an *interest proration?*

When you borrow money on a mortgage, you pay interest in arrears—you owe it at the end of each month of borrowing. By comparison, when you rent property, you normally pay your rent in advance, at the beginning of each month. That means that when you obtain a mortgage to buy a property, there's going to be a partial month before a payment is due. For example, if the month has 30 days and you close on the 20th, you will owe 10 days' worth of interest at the end of that first month. Then your regular monthly payment would begin at the end of the following month. However, it is awkward for lenders to collect a third of a month's interest. So they have you pay it in advance at the time the escrow closes. This appears as a prorated interest charge on your closing statement. It is a normal charge. However, you may want to do your own calculations to be sure the amount you are being charged is accurate. *Note:* This is a charge for *interest only.* It is not simply a fraction of your monthly payment, for which you would normally pay both principal and interest.

What is a *judgment payoff?*

This fee is normally charged only to sellers or those who are refinancing. When you are purchasing (or selling) a home, judgments against you rarely show up. These may be from unpaid bills from a long time ago, from a civil suit, or from some other action taken against you that rendered a money decision in someone else's favor and resulted in a lien on the property. They can be for small or large sums of money. Very often these are from the forgotten past and suddenly show up like ghosts. Nevertheless, when they appear, they must usually be paid off before a lender will agree to give you a new mortgage. Therefore, they may appear on your closing statement as a payoff. You should have been forewarned about them by the escrow officer or your real estate agent or both. Learning about them in advance will give you time to examine them to determine if you truly owe them or they are a mistake. And if they are a mistake, you can contact the entity they are from and see that they are removed. Otherwise, in order to get the loan to close the deal, you may have to make the payoff. *If you are a borrower and see a judgment charge on your closing costs, be sure to determine if it was mistakenly placed there and belongs, instead, on the seller's closing sheet.*

What are the *lender's legal fees?*

You may have an attorney as part of your team to help you close the deal on the house you are buying. You would expect to pay the attorney for his or her services, and that is covered in the next chapter. However, the lender may also have an attorney who checks over the lender's documents to be sure they are appropriate and valid. Here the lender is charging you for its attorney's work. To my way of thinking, this is a garbage fee *unless* there was something special about the mortgage that you obtained that required unusual legal work. For example, special legal work is often required for closing commercial or industrial property sales. For the run-of-the-mill home sale, however, the lender's attorney's fees are pretty much standardized, and I feel that they are a usual and necessary part of doing business. And they should be absorbed by the lender, not you.

What is a *loan discount fee?*

To get a lower interest rate on your mortgage, you may have agreed to pay a discount fee. These fees are expressed as points. One point is equivalent to 1 percent of the loan amount. For example, on a $200,000 mortgage, a 2-point discount would be $4000. It is, in effect, prepaid interest. You should have been made aware of this charge at the time you obtained your financing; hence its appearance on your closing statement should be no surprise. The good news is that this discount fee could be deductible from your income taxes as an interest deduction. You should check with your accountant to find out if you qualify for this.

What is a *loan escrow fee?*

As part of closing a real estate transaction, you will normally open an escrow. The escrow company is an independent third party, typically a licensed corporation, that handles all money and documents. However, sometimes in addition to the regular escrow, the lender may require a second independent *loan escrow*. This is often the case when you are applying for a special type of mortgage, for example, a *blanket loan* covering several properties. The loan escrow and the property escrow run concurrently and usually close simultaneously. However, there is a separate fee for the loan escrow, and it may appear on your closing statement. Usually you are told if the lender will require a separate loan escrow at the time the regular escrow account is opened. That's the time to negotiate its cost. Some lenders are willing to absorb part of the cost of this separate escrow, and some escrow companies, if asked, will reduce its cost.

What is a *loan lock fee*?

Many borrowers will want to lock in the interest rate on their mortgage at the time they apply. This is particularly the case when the mortgage market is volatile and there is concern that rates might rise during the month or so between application for a mortgage and actual closing. Sometimes these lock-ins are free. But other times, the lender may charge typically one-eighth to one-quarter of 1 point. If the loan lock fee is one-eighth of 1 point and the mortgage is for $200,000, the fee is $250. If you agreed to pay this fee for a loan lock at the time you applied for your mortgage, then you can expect it to show up on your closing statement. Be sure, however, that the amount has been calculated correctly. If rates drop by the time escrow closes, it may be possible to switch to a new lender to avoid paying the loan lock fee.

What is a *loan origination fee*?

This charge is similar to the discount fee. However, technically it is not an interest charge. Rather, it is a fee to the lender for originating the loan that you are obtaining. Going back several decades, the FHA came up with the term. When a borrower obtained an FHA loan in the 1950s, for example, the lender could charge 1 percent for the mortgage for its costs in dealing with the FHA. This became known as the "origination fee." Later, lenders applied this fee to other loans as well. My feeling is that although it sounds very official, unless you're getting an FHA loan, it's probably a garbage fee. In today's market, lenders roll all of their costs into the interest rate on your mortgage and the discount (discussed above). An origination fee is a fancy way of adding an additional amount of money for you to pay. Also, check with your accountant for current tax rules—it may not be deductible.

What is a *loan payoff*?

When you pay off an existing mortgage, as is the case if you are the seller or are refinancing, the lender sends a demand to escrow for the amount to pay off the principal plus any remaining interest. The payoff demand also includes any fees, penalties, or other charges that are owed on the loan. If the loan is in default, these charges can be substantial. The payoff demand is based on an estimated closing date that the escrow officer gives to the lender. If it takes longer to close than the estimate, you'll be charged loan-payoff interest (described below). If it's shorter, you could get some interest back after the close of escrow. The loan payoff is a normal and necessary seller's loan charge, and it pays for the lender's services in paying off the existing mortgage on the property. *If you are a borrower and see a loan payoff charge on your closing costs, be sure to determine if it was mistakenly placed there rather than on the seller's closing sheet.*

What is *loan payoff interest* (proration)?

This is also a charge normally to a seller. If you already own a property and are doing a refinance, then it will be a charge to you. As noted above under "interest proration," interest on real estate loans is paid in arrears, at the end of each month. Therefore, when you are paying off a mortgage, there will usually be some interest due from your last payment until escrow closes. For example, if your last payment was on the first of March and you close escrow on the 16th, you will owe 16 days of interest. The lender will calculate this amount and add it into the payoff demand (see below) it sends to escrow. But, for reasons unforeseen, you may not close until March 20. Now you owe an additional 4 days. The escrow officer will calculate how much this is on a prorated basis and charge it to you as part of your closing costs. It's simply the remainder that you owe on paying off your old mortgage. *If you are a borrower and see a loan payoff proration charge on your closing costs, be sure to determine if it was mistakenly placed there rather than on the seller's closing sheet.*

What are *loan processing fees?*

This is a kind of grab bag of fees that can include charges for the following services:

- The lender or mortgage broker pays to have one of the country's secondary lenders (Fannie Mae or Freddie Mac) give an opinion (underwriting) as to the worthiness of the loan. This fee is passed on to the buyer as part of the loan processing fees. The fee for this service is typically around $100, and I consider it a normal part of doing business for the lender.

- The time it takes to assemble all of the documents necessary to complete the loan package is often paid for as part of the loan processing fees. Often the loan broker will charge this fee in order to be paid for his or her time and efforts. Be aware, however, that in most cases the loan broker is being paid a handsome fee outside of escrow from the lender for acquiring you as a borrower, and hence, to my way of thinking, this work that he or she does should be included in that other fee. *Note:* HUD is considering making it mandatory that loan brokers openly list the amount of the fee they get from lenders.

- A lender may charge a fee for going through the motions of giving you financing. It can include preparing the loan documents (although that can be a separate fee), verifying your credit, income, and cash balances, or almost anything else. Usually these are what I consider to be garbage fees.

What is a *miscellaneous loan fee?*

Although your escrow officer will undoubtedly try to be completely accurate in your closing statement, sometimes it will not be possible to determine exactly all of the costs at the time the deal closes. Therefore, a small fund is usually set aside to cover any unexpected costs that arise. Typically this amount is a few hundred dollars. If no unexpected fees crop up, you can expect to receive most of it back in the form of a check from the escrow company a few days after the closing.

What is a *mortgage insurance application fee?*

Whenever you get financing that is for 80 percent or more of the value of the property you are buying, you will be required to get mortgage insurance. This is insurance from a private company that insures not you but the lender for a certain percentage of loss in the event that you fail to make your mortgage payments and the lender must foreclose. Of course, you will be making the premium payments (usually around 0.5 percent or somewhat higher) each month as part of your regular mortgage payment. However, in order to get this mortgage insurance, the lender must apply for it. And there may be an application fee. Here, the lender is passing that fee onto you. To my way of thinking, this should be a normal part of doing business for the lender, and it should absorb the fee.

What is a *nonrecurring cost* (NRCC)?

Some fees may be lumped together under this heading, particularly if the seller is paying them for you. *Nonrecurring* means that they are simply one-time charges. Termite or home inspection fees are nonrecurring as are escrow and title insurance costs. In contrast, interest, taxes, and insurance are normally considered recurring costs. Here, you will want to be sure that the charges are, in fact, accurate. You may want to take out the documentation you received from your insurance agent, for example, to see that you are being charged the correct amount. *Note:* Sometimes these fees are estimates, particularly when the escrow officer has not yet received final demand statements. Therefore, the insurance fee, for example, may be labeled as an "estimate," and it may be higher than your insurance agent told you it would be. You should receive a check for the difference after escrow closes.

CHAPTER TWO

What is a *photo fee?*

There are several times during the sale and closing of a home that it may be photographed. Early on the real estate agent may photograph it for the purpose of putting it in a listing as well as on give-away brochures. The appraiser will take a photo of the property as part of his or her appraisal report. The insurance agent will usually want a photo as part of the insurance package. And so on. Sometimes a fee for any of these photo shoots could show up as part of the closing. To my way of thinking, any photos taken by lenders, insurers, appraisers, or others are part of their normal course of doing business, and you should not have to pay for them. On the other hand, if you order a photographer out to take a picture of the property for your own purposes, you can expect to pay the costs. *Note:* Many people who take photos, such as appraisers and insurance agents, will insist that these be Polaroids, which are much harder to digitally alter or "improve."

What is a *point?*

When a loan is discounted, the amount of the discount is listed in points. It is 1 percent of the total mortgage value. For example, if the mortgage is for $300,000 and there are 3 points, they are equal to $9000. Points are a fee that can show up on escrow closing statements. They are usually first seen when you apply for the mortgage. It might be expressed as 7 percent plus 3 points. That means that the interest rate will be 7 percent and the loan is discounted to you by 3 percent. (You'll have to come up with 3 percent of it out of your pocket.) You want to be sure that the points expressed when you first apply for the mortgage are the same as are charged to you when you get your closing statement. (*Note:* With most lenders it is usually possible to decrease the points by increasing the interest rate slightly or to decrease the interest rate by increasing the points, usually significantly.)

What is a *prepayment penalty fee?*

This is a charge normally to a seller or to someone who is refinancing a loan. It is a penalty for paying off the existing loan earlier. It usually shows up in the closing cost statement. The amount can be minimal, a few hundred dollars, or quite significant, for example, 6 months' worth of interest. It is worth your while as part of your strategy for obtaining a new loan to determine if it has a built-in prepayment penalty. If it does, you may want to opt for a mortgage that does not have one. In today's marketplace, lenders will sometimes offer you a small bonus or a slightly lower interest rate if you are willing to accept a prepayment penalty as part of your new loan.

If you are a borrower and see a prepayment charge on your closing costs, be sure to determine if it was mistakenly placed there and belongs, instead, on the seller's closing sheet.

What is a *prorated tax?*

Property taxes are assessed on an annual basis, although they are typically due twice a year. In California, for example, the first half of the property taxes are due November 1 (with a December 10 deadline) and March 1 (with an April 10 deadline). When you buy property, assuming that the taxes are to be prorated, the sellers owe taxes during that period of time that they owned the property. You owe for the time you own the property. Thus, depending on the date when you buy and when the taxes were actually paid, the sellers may owe you taxes that were due but not yet paid. Or you may owe taxes to them that were paid but not yet due. The difference is paid out to whoever owes based on a per day ownership of the property. For example, if you owe the sellers for 30 days of taxes they had already paid and the annual taxes were $3600, you would have a charge of $300. Keep in mind, however, that this is neither a bonus nor a gift to the sellers. Rather, you are only paying them back for the amount they prepaid on taxes during your period of ownership.

What is a *settlement* or *closing fee?*

This can be a charge for a lender's escrow, in which case, as long as it's for a reasonable amount, it would be a normal fee. On the other hand, it could be a charge that a lender may impose for providing settlement documents for closing your escrow. It's tantamount to charging you for a sales slip when you purchase something in a store, and it's certainly a charge I would question.

What is a *supplemental tax?*

In many states the property is reassessed at the time of purchase. However, this reassessment is often done well after the initial tax bill is sent. Therefore, there may be a notice on your closing statement that a supplemental tax bill will be coming. For example, you may pay $1000 in taxes that are due at the time you purchase your home. However, at a later date when the property is reassessed (based on the closing date), the taxes are higher than the amount you paid. You will then receive a supplemental tax bill for that extra amount. Typically you can pay it either immediately or at your next regular tax installment due date.

What is a *tax lien?*

Taxes are considered a lien (something involving money that ties up or encumbers the title) on property. In California, for example, a lien for taxes is placed on a property as of January 1 of the year preceding the state's fiscal year (July 1 to June 30). If taxes have not been paid by the time they are due, an actual tax lien is placed on the property that prevents the sellers from providing clear title, and the lender will not give you a loan until the title is cleared. In addition, there can be tax liens from other sources. For example, the IRS can place a lien on property as can other government taxing agencies. Again, until these liens are cleared, no clear title can be given and no loan will be forthcoming. Normally, it is the job of the seller to pay off and clear these tax liens. However, depending on the deal you negotiated, you may have agreed to pay some of the seller's closing costs, such as these liens. (This often happens when you're buying property in a foreclosure, for example.) Thus, the amount of the tax lien will crop up as an expense on your closing statement. Be sure the amount stated is correct—you've verified it with the taxing agency. You certainly don't want to overpay!

What is a *tax service fee?*

Almost all mortgages provide that if you don't make your tax payments in a timely fashion, the lender can step in

and make the payments for you. Why would a mortgage company do this? To protect its mortgage. What typically happens if you don't pay is that the lender makes the tax payment, and then adds the amount plus penalties and costs to your mortgage. And then the lender may call the mortgage or, in other words, begin foreclosure. (You don't want to skip your tax payments!) However, in order for all of this to happen, the lender has to know that you have not made your tax payments. Since many lenders are out of state, keeping track could be quite difficult. However, there are companies set up to do nothing but look for tax liens placed on property for failure to pay. As soon as they discover one, they notify the lender, who then goes through the procedure outlined above. For this service the company charges a nominal fee, typically under $50. This is a fee you are normally expected to pay—a tax service fee. While it can be argued that this also should be simply a cost of doing business, having buyers pay the fee is long established in the industry, so don't expect to easily get out of it.

What is a *termite and fungus clearance certificate fee?*

This is a charge that a termite inspection firm will make for issuing a certificate stating that your property is infestation free. It is usually issued after any remedial work that was required has been completed. Some states have a specific form that must be used. Almost no lender will fund a mortgage until this certificate is deposited in escrow. (It assures lenders that the property isn't likely to fall down soon because of termite or fungus damage.) The cost of the certificate itself is usually minimal. However, since it's usually the obligation of the seller to provide a home free and clear of infestation, it's usually the seller who pays this fee. Check to be sure that it hasn't accidentally been put into your closing statement.

What is a *termite and fungus inspection fee?*

This is the inspection of the property by a state-licensed termite and fungus inspector to determine if there is any infestation. Normally, the seller pays for this. However, in some states it is not uncommon for the buyer to pay for it

while the seller pays for any corrective work that is deemed necessary. The cost is usually between $200 and $300. If you are asked to pay for it, you should have been given the opportunity to shop for the best price from an inspection firm. If the seller doesn't like the results, he or she is free to hire, and pay for, another inspection. The key is obtaining a clearance certificate (see above), and as long as it's from a state-licensed firm, the lender usually won't object to the source or to what work is done.

What is a *termite and fungus work fee?*

This is a charge for work done on a property involving termite and fungus infestation. Although the determination of who does the work and who pays for it is up for negotiation, in most purchases the seller pays for fixing any damage done by termites or fungus. This work must usually be completed before a termite clearance certificate (see above) is issued. On the other hand, the buyer usually has the option of having and paying for any preventative work. This might involve such things as regrading, removing structural boards that come in contact with the ground, using certain chemicals to kill termites that might be in the soil, and so forth. Typically it's optional. But, if you opt to have the work done, you'll need to pay for it. Presumably, you have talked with the company doing the work and have settled on a price. You should check to be sure that the amount be charged to you in escrow is the price you had agreed upon.

What is an *underwriting fee?*

Depending on the amount of your mortgage, you could be getting a *conforming loan.* (The amount varies, but today the maximum conforming loan is for $327,200.) *Conforming* means that your loan will conform to the standards of the two giant secondary financial institutions in the United States, Fannie Mae and Freddie Mac. The lender who actually gives you your loan typically will package it with others and sell it to these organizations. However, before ever loaning you the money, your lender wants to be sure that the loan will be purchased. Therefore, it has Fannie Mae or Freddie Mac actually look it over and approve it (underwrite it). Your loan application

and whatever other documentation is needed actually goes to one of these two lenders who then typically gives a provisional okay, provided you do any number of things (such as slightly increase the down payment, demonstrate additional income, clear some debt, and so on) to satisfy them. Today it's handled electronically and can be done in a matter of a few hours. However, there is a cost to the lender for this underwriting service. This is the source of the underwriting fee that is being passed along to you. Some say it's a reasonable cost for the buyer to pay. Once again, however, to my way of thinking, it's simply a cost of doing business and should be borne by the lender.

What is a *warehousing fee*?

A *warehouse* is a place where you store goods until you are ready to sell them. It applies, or used to, to mortgage money as well as to shoes and cheese. When you are applying for a loan, say, $500,000, to purchase a home, you want that money to be available to you when it's time to close escrow. However, the lender wants that money to be out there earning interest. Typically lenders have a limited amount of capital with which to work. Most is in play in the form of mortgages. Some is coming from mortgages being paid off and interest received. And some is going out in the form of funding for new mortgages (yours, for example). For the lender, handling all of this cash flow so that the money is always in circulation can be a nightmare. So, in the days before computers and wire transfers, lenders would often "store" money in a warehouse (actually a bank) for a few days to be sure it was available when you needed it. The warehousing fee is the lender's charge to you for having your loan money ready to go when you call for it. However, today warehousing is somewhat obsolete. Because money is transferred electronically, it is possible for it to generate interest not only on a daily basis but hourly and in some cases, minute to minute. However, that money may generate only a small amount of interest in a bank as opposed to 5 or 7 or more percent as a mortgage. Hence, again the warehousing fee. Nevertheless, to my way of thinking, this is a cost of doing business for the lender who has no business charging the borrower for it.

What is a *wire transfer fee?*

As we noted, funds are often transferred electronically today. Sometimes, however, there is a fee for doing this. If it's the lender's money, then you shouldn't be charged for the transfer unless there are special circumstances in which you need the money sooner—or later—than anticipated. If the fee is for the transfer of your own money, say, the down payment to escrow, then it's a normal and necessary charge.

What is a *yield spread fee?*

Often you will have your mortgage interest rate quoted at a certain rate. However, by the time you close your loan, your rates may have gone up. For example, you may have been quoted a 6.5 percent loan only to discover upon closing that the actual interest rate is 7 percent. Normally, the mortgage papers will reflect the new interest rate. However, in the case of a "lock" (see page 26), you may be entitled to the original (6.5 percent) quoted. Thus, the lender is actually losing money. It may try to gain some of this money back by charging you a fee in the form of points for the spread in yield between the lock and the market rate. This is definitely a no-no, especially if you already paid a fee for the lock.

3

Title Insurance and Escrow Closing Costs

QUESTIONS TO ASK YOURSELF

What is *title insurance?*

Title insurance is similar to other types of insurance in that it protects the insured against financial loss. For example, you pay a premium to buy a life insurance policy so that if you die during the term of the policy's coverage, your beneficiaries will receive money from the insurance company. Similarly, you pay a premium to buy a health insurance policy so that if you get sick during the term of the policy's coverage, you, or others covered, will receive money from the insurance company. When you pay a premium to buy a title insurance policy, if problems arise related to the title to the property covered by the policy, the insurance company pays you money to compensate for financial losses caused by the title defect that was not "cured" prior to your purchasing the property and assuming its title.

The one-time premium you are charged for this protection is the title insurance fee that appears on your closing statement. The insurance, depending on how extensive the coverage is that you buy, will take care of such things as recorded but not discovered liens, improper recording of deeds, and in some cases even property-line disputes.

When does title insurance protection begin and end?

A life insurance policy protects the insured against events that occur any time after the moment the policy is purchased. In contrast, a title insurance policy protects the insured against any losses arising from events that took place prior to the time the policy took effect. It works backward covering you (or the lender) against title problems in the past. It extends back indefinitely.

For how long am I covered by the title insurance?

The answer is almost indefinitely. As long as you own the property or have any interest in it or have any obligation to it, you should be protected. In some cases this coverage may continue to be in force even after you sell the property. But keep in mind, the protection covers you only for events that occurred prior to your buying the title insurance—in other words, for events prior to the time you owned the property. It does not cover you for any events that might occur after you buy the policy. For example, if you don't pay your local property taxes and a lien is consequently placed on your property, your title insurance policy will be no help in removing the lien.

Why do I have to pay title insurance fees?

Title insurance is not a legal requirement for purchasing a home. However, no lender I've ever heard of will give you a mortgage unless you have it. (If you don't have clear title, the mortgage could be invalid and the lender could lose.) And any buyer who has common sense would want it to protect his or her equity in the property. Therefore, you *may* have to pay for it. Who pays for title insurance is a matter of custom in your area. In some areas the seller pays it. In other areas, it's a cost to the buyer. In many cases the fee is split. Who pays for it can also be a matter of negotiation in the sale. See also "shopping around" below.

What is an *escrow holder?*

An *escrow holder* (an independent third party) serves the other parties involved in a property transfer by handling all the money and relevant documents that pertain to the transfer. In real estate the escrow holder collects and holds onto the money (deposit, down payment, mortgage, and fees) from the buyer and the signed deed from the seller. The holder handles other documents as well, such as loan papers, that are necessary to conclude the deal. When the escrow holder deems that the terms of the deal have been met completely or perfectly, it transfers the money it is holding to the appropriate people (seller, taxing agency, lien holder, and so on) and records the deed in favor of you, the buyer. In most states there are licensed companies that have been created for the sole purpose of handling escrow accounts. In some parts of the East Coast, attorneys rather than escrow companies may provide escrow services.

Why do I have to pay escrow fees?

As is true of title insurance, it is not a legal requirement to have an escrow account when purchasing a home. You could simply hand the money over to the sellers, and they could hand you a deed. However, that's a "messy" way of doing things. The sellers might not be sure they were getting everything to which they were entitled. You might not be sure you were getting a valid deed. In addition, you will want to be confident that all of the terms of the property transfer are being met as you near the closing date. That assurance can be had most easily from an escrow company whose job it is to accumulate the documents and funds from the different parties involved in the transfer. Further, no lender I've ever heard of will give you a mortgage unless you establish an escrow. You *may* have to pay for the escrow services. Whether the seller or buyer is responsible for paying for escrow services is usually subject to the prevailing local customs. In some areas the seller pays it, and in other areas, the buyer pays it. In many cases the fee is split. Or it can be determined by negotiation. You should find out if it will be a cost to you when you open the escrow account, and you should shop around for the company that offers the most reasonable rates.

Can escrow or title fees be excessive?

Sometimes, and this is increasingly becoming a problem. Since these fees are largely unregulated, a few independent title and escrow companies in some states have taken to boosting their fees up into the stratosphere. I've seen buyers shocked at the closing when they discover that they owe thousands more to an escrow company than they anticipated. While the industry is working hard to regulate itself, it's important not to get caught by an unscrupulous company. Since it's usually far too late to complain the day before closing (when you'll get your HUD-1, or final closing instructions), it's important to shop around for the best prices from escrow companies *before* opening an account. *Note:* If you're paying for the escrow, don't let anyone, including your agent or the seller, demand that you use a particular escrow company if that company's prices are exorbitant. Remember that some real estate agencies are aligned with escrow companies and that the main reason they may want you to deal with the company they recommend is to throw business its way.

Does someone get a kickback or referral fee ("controlled business")?

In general, you need to pay a fee only if a service for it was actually performed, although the amount is negotiable. Kickbacks or referral fees are generally prohibited. However, there is a special status called a *controlled,* or *affiliated, business arrangement* whereby the party referring the home buyer to a provider of services has a relationship with that provider that involves an ownership or franchise. This sometimes happens when a real estate company wants you to use its internal title insurance and escrow services. This is allowed provided that the controlled business arrangement is disclosed, you're given a written estimate of costs by the provider of the service, and you are not required to use that service. Occasionally the fact that you are not required to use the controlled service can be overlooked. Sometimes the dubious argument is made that only the controlled escrow and/or title company can be trusted to handle your deal. Keep in mind that most escrow and title companies are state licensed.

Should I shop for title insurance companies to find the one that charges the lowest fee?

Perhaps. It depends on where you live. Some states, such as Texas and New Mexico, regulate fees so they will be the same for any title company. New York, New Jersey, Pennsylvania, Ohio, and other states have a single rate schedule for all carriers. Other states do not regulate rates at all, such as Georgia, Alabama, Washington, D.C., Hawaii, Indiana, Illinois, Oklahoma, West Virginia, and Massachusetts. If you live in a state not mentioned, then you should check out the available title insurance carriers because the rate will tend to vary company to company. *Note:* Under HUD settlement procedures rules, the seller may not require, as a condition of sale, that title insurance be purchased by the buyer from any particular title company. (In theory, if the seller violates this rule, he or she could be liable to you for up to three times all charges made for the title insurance!) Checking out rates can be done simply by calling different companies. If you tell them the purchase price of the property, they should be able to quickly give you a fairly accurate estimate of their charges. If you decide to go with them, be sure you get their estimate in writing.

Who calculates the escrow and title insurance fees that I have to pay?

Typically the escrow company representative will draw up two sets of closing instructions: preliminary and final. The preliminary given to you shortly after escrow is opened will estimate your closing costs. The final will be the actual figures (or very close to them) and will be given to you at least 1 day before escrow closes, and they will include a HUD-1 form. It's important that you understand that both sets of closing instructions are based on the purchase agreement that you signed. Since sometimes the terms of this agreement can be a matter of interpretation, it's very important that you check the closing statements, especially the preliminary agreement, to be sure they reflect the exact intent of the purchase agreement. It's not uncommon for an escrow officer to misinterpret a term. If this is done, and you don't catch it in time, it could cost you hundreds if not thousands of dollars. Be wary of extra costs added in such as commissions and transaction fees.

How do I open escrow?

Actually, your agent will probably do this for you, although it's quite simple. Once you've shopped for the best escrow company, you simply show up with your purchase agreement and ask that they handle an escrow for the sale. They will be most happy to comply. They will study your purchase agreement and based on what it says, draw up "preliminary escrow instructions." Read this carefully to be sure there aren't extra charges, such as a transaction fee to an agent, attached. (See Chapter 13.) This document tells the escrow holder or officer what to do in order to complete the transaction, or close escrow. Be sure you want to go through with the deal when you sign this agreement because these agreements also usually contain a clause stating that you will pay for the service whether or not the deal actually concludes! (In many cases as a matter of good will, the charges are waived if the deal falls through.)

What does the escrow holder do?

As soon as the escrow account is opened, the escrow officer will start working on the following:

- Prepare preliminary instructions (as noted above).
- Order a title search (to see who owns the property and how it is encumbered).
- Request demands or beneficiary statements (from any lenders of record so the seller can see who has to be paid off to give clear title).
- Accept loan instructions from your lender.
- Accept all reports (such as termite clearances).
- Accept a fire insurance policy and any other required insurance policies.
- Demand funds from your lender.
- Record the title to you.
- Close the escrow account by paying funds to the seller, paying off the existing lender(s) and other lien holders, and delivering all the documents.

QUESTIONS TO ASK YOUR ESCROW AND/OR TITLE INSURANCE OFFICER

What is the *abstract-of-title-search fee?*

In order to sell a property, the sellers have to establish that they have clear title to it. The way this is done in modern times is to conduct a search of property records. Theoretically this search goes back historically to the first owner. In the West, for example, it often goes back to the Spanish land grants issued hundreds of years ago. As a practical matter, however, most title searches go back only to the last clear title search. For example, if the property was previously sold 5 years ago with a clear title, the new search goes back for 5 years. For that period of time the records are searched for any new liens or other encumbrances placed on the property. An *encumbrance* is anything that affects the title. It could be a money judgment (lien), a utility company right-of-way, or an encroachment by a neighbor building a home on a part of the property. An *abstract of title* is a summary of all the items that have affected the title. Any problems, or "clouds," on the title will show up in the abstract, and the seller can then make an effort to have them removed. Of course, there is a fee for the search and the abstract.

What is the *prorated adjustment for taxes?*

While real estate is still not subject to state sales taxes (in any jurisdiction I know of), there are state and/or local town or city property taxes to pay. (And there may be a transfer tax imposed by the city, county, or state.) Your closing statement may reflect your fair share of the property taxes sometimes shown as an adjustment. When you buy property, normally the sellers owe property taxes for the period of time that they owned the property. You owe for the time you own the property. Thus, depending on the date when you close the deal and the date when the sellers actually paid the taxes, the sellers may owe you money for taxes that are due but not yet paid. Or you may owe the sellers money for taxes they paid ahead of the tax payment due date. The difference is paid out to the buyer or seller, as appropriate, on a per-day basis.

What is an *ALTA fee?*

American Land Title Association (ALTA) is a higher form of title insurance that lenders may demand. It involves someone from the title insurance company actually going out to the property and determining that a house is on it, that the boundaries are correct, and that any other features listed as part of the property are indeed on the property. This extra title insurance is sometimes called a *lender's title.* Since it gives extra protection (to the lender), there is an extra fee charged. If the lender demands the policy, you will have to get it—and pay for it. As always, be sure you shop around for the best rates.

What is an *association fee?*

If you are buying a condominium, townhouse, co-op, or single-family home that's part of an association, you may owe two fees. The first may be a prorata charge for your portion of the monthly (quarterly or annual) home owners' association charges. For example, if you buy on October 1 and the annual dues of $1200 were due and payable in June, you would owe the sellers 3 months' worth (October, November, and December) of home owner's fees that the sellers had paid in advance, or $300. The second fee may be a charge that many home owners' associations make for giving you a package that typically includes the following:

- *Conditions, covenants, and restrictions (CCR).* This is a document that runs with the title and governs the home owners' association.
- *Bylaws.* These are the governing rules adopted by the home owners' association.
- *Regulations.* These are typically the association's rules governing usage of common facilities. For example, members may use the pool and spa only between the hours of 10 in the morning and 9 at night, or there is no overnight parking in guest parking zones.
- *A list of pertinent legal action(s).* This is a comprehensive list of the legal actions that the home owners' association is currently or was previ-

ously involved in. It includes all actions, even
those that were settled in the past.

This package would also include any other documents
that are relevant to your ownership.

In the past, many home owners' associations would
refuse to disclose this information claiming privacy rights.
But laws in many states now require disclosure to new
purchasers. However, the home owners' association can
charge a fee, typically a couple of hundred dollars, for the
package.

What are *attorneys' fees?*

There may be fees for several attorneys, and those fees
should be broken down so that you can easily see whom
you are paying what:

- *Your attorney.* If you hired an attorney to help
  you either in the negotiations or the closing, his
  or her fee should show up here. You will want to
  verify that the charge is the same as you originally agreed upon.

- *Lender's attorney.* The lender may charge you a
  fee for its attorney's services. Since the lender's
  attorney, presumably, represents the lender, not
  you, it is a questionable fee. Many people,
  including me, consider this a garbage fee thrown
  in to increase the mortgage yield to the lender.
  You should discuss this fee and try to have it dis-
  missed when you apply for the mortgage. (See
  also Chapter 2.)

- *Title and/or escrow company attorney.* If your transaction required some special legal treatment,
  such as a difficult-to-execute deed or a legal
  opinion on a part of the title, the fee will be
  shown here. If you requested the service, as long
  as the fee isn't unreasonable, you should expect
  to pay for it. On the other hand, if you didn't
  require any special legal services and this is a
  general cost for the escrow and/or title insurance company's attorney, then it's probably a
  garbage fee and should be disputed.

What is the *check remittance fee?*

Occasionally this will crop up. It's usually a fee for special handling of a check. For example, if your down payment check was drawn on an out-of-state bank, but the escrow required the money overnight, a fee might be charged for expediting the cashing of the check. As long as the amount is not unreasonable and it was for a service actually performed, you should expect to pay it.

What is the *contract sales price?*

This is the price you are paying for your home as shown on your purchase agreement. It is important that you verify that the amount shown on your preliminary and final closing documents reflects this price accurately. Since virtually all other fees are in some way influenced by this figure, if it's off, the amount that you owe could be off as well.

What is the *document preparation fee?*

Many escrow companies simply charge a flat fee for escrow services. If they do, then it's fairly easy for you to compare the fee with the fees of other companies to find the best deal. Some companies, however, break down their services. One of the inclusive fees they typically will charge is for document preparation. Since there are relatively few documents, outside of the mortgage, for you as a buyer to sign (unless your deal requires something special), this is a strange fee. It presumably covers the paperwork that the escrow company prepares for you, such as creating the closing statements and any other closing documents not prepared by the lender. To my way of thinking, it can be a garbage fee designed to inflate the money that's going to the escrow company. If your escrow company breaks its charge down into separate fees, add them all up together to get its final fee and use that to comparison shop. If an escrow company gave you a written estimate of the fee it would charge at the time it opened the escrow account and the final charge is inflated by a lot of garbage fees, I would certainly challenge it.

What is the *escrow fee?*

This is the charge that the escrow company is making for running the escrow account for you. According to custom or negotiation, it can be charged either to the seller, to you the buyer, or split between the two of you. The escrow company should be able to give you a highly accurate written estimate of this fee at the time you open escrow. You should use that estimate to shop around for the lowest possible fees.

What are *express letter fees?*

In order to close your escrow, it may be necessary to send (or receive) some documents at great distance. For example, if you have an out-of-state relative cosigning on the mortgage (to help you qualify), that person will need to sign all the loan documents. Rather than have him or her come all the way to your escrow office, the documents will be expressed to the person's home or office and back. Of course, you can expect to be charged the mailing fees. Be aware, however, that these rarely go through the U.S. Post Office. More likely, they'll go via FedEx, UPS Blue or Red Label, DHL, or some similar service. The fees for these services are typically around $15 or $20 per letter; however, for companies who send express letters on a regular basis, the prices of such shipments are deeply discounted. The escrow company may figure that it costs a bit more because they have to run someone down to drop it in the express mailbox (most express companies pick up for a negligible fee), so they may add on to the costs. If the fees are more than $25 per letter, you may want to question them.

What is a *forwarding and/or demand fee?*

This is a charge by your escrow company for demanding that your loan company forward the loan funds to it. To close your escrow, the lender must transfer the amount of the mortgage to it. However, lenders don't let their money sit idly in escrow accounts. They want it earning interest at all times. Hence, they won't send it until they get a demand from the escrow company, and that demand usually states that the escrow is complete or perfect, missing only the loan. At that time, the lender will usually send the funds electronically to the escrow company's fiduciary account. Thus, the forwarding and/or demand fee is a charge to you typically from the escrow company for their services in demanding the funds. Unless problems arise—for example, the escrow company must demand the funds many times before getting them—this should be just another case of doing business and covered by the flat rate. In other words, it's probably a garbage fee and should be covered under the overall escrow charges.

What is the *lender's escrow fee?*

The lender may require a separate escrow. This is often the case when there is more than one loan on the property or the loan is a specialty loan such as a "blanket mortgage" covering several properties. The lender wants to be sure that all the work required to secure its loan is handled separately and not confused with the general transfer of title. Of course, you'll be expected to pay this fee. Your lender should have told you it would require a separate escrow, and you should have shopped around for the lowest fees *before* opening your escrow account for the lender.

What are *nonrecurring closing cost credits and debits?*

Nonrecurring closing costs (NRCC) are one-time charges. An NRCC *credit* to you means that someone else is paying these charges for you. An NRCC *debit* means that you are paying them for someone else. Some examples of NRCC charges are points on your mortgage, title insurance, and escrow fees. (Closing costs that recur are such things as interest on your mortgage, taxes, and insurance payments—they accrue on an ongoing basis and are payable monthly or annually.) Some lenders will allow the seller to pay some or all of the buyer's NRCC, but other lenders will prohibit anyone else from paying a buyer's NRCC feeling that if the buyer needs someone else to pay the charges, he or she may be a poor risk.

What is a *personal property debit?*

When you buy a home, the land and the house on it are considered *real property,* or *real estate.* However, items that can be easily removed by the seller without damaging the property are considered *personal property.* Personal property consists of furniture, clothing, some fixtures and appliances, and other things. Sometimes you may want to buy some of the seller's personal property in addition to purchasing the house. For example, you may wish to purchase the seller's refrigerator. Since moving a refrigerator is an expensive proposition (and sometimes results in breaking it), oftentimes the seller is receptive to the idea and may be willing to sell it to you at a bargain basement price. Hence, you may find a $50 debit for personal property on your closing costs that refers to your purchase of the refrigerator. Most real estate agents know, however, that it's best to keep personal property transactions out of the real estate purchase agreement to avoid any complications with the lender. Hence, you may end up paying $50 to the seller out of pocket for the refrigerator and never see it mentioned on your closing instructions.

What is a *settlement charge?*

This is usually the amount of money that you or the seller must come up with to close the escrow. In your case, as the buyer, it usually equals the deposit plus the down payment plus all of the closing costs. For the seller it's usually just the closing costs, which are taken out of the receipts from the sale.

What is a *short payoff fund?*

Sometimes you can get a bargain in real estate by buying a property from a seller who is *upside down.* This means that the amount he or she owes on the property is higher than the property's actual market value. The question becomes, how can you sell a property for less than you owe? The answer is that the lender must be willing to accept less than the full mortgage amount. In bad markets with a seller in foreclosure, some lenders are willing to do this. (Check in my book *How to Find Hidden Real Estate*

Bargains for tips on how to get lenders to go along with that type of suggestion.) If you're the buyer in this situation, you may be required to put the money from your new loan, down payment, and deposit into a fund, all of which (after expenses) will go to the existing lender on the property. From that fund will be deducted enough to pay for the seller's closing costs (that the lender agrees to) when the deal closes. In these sorts of transactions, the seller typically does not get any money out of the property but instead feels lucky to get rid of the home and retain some part of his or her good credit.

What is a *survey fee?*

There are two types of survey fees. In one case you've hired a surveyor to go out to the property to stake the boundaries. This is always a good idea and is usually a real necessity in rural areas or where there are irregular lots. Of course, the surveyor will submit a bill, which is considered a survey fee. On the other hand, the title insurance company may send its own representatives out to survey the property to be sure there actually is a house on it and that the boundaries are well defined. Here you are being charged separately for this service, probably in addition to a lender's title insurance policy.

What are *tax stamp fees?*

When buying property, some jurisdictions will tax the transfer. This is technically called a *documentary transfer tax*. In California, for example, the state tax is computed at the rate of 55 cents for each $500 of consideration (or fraction). Cities, counties, and other jurisdictions may also require a transfer tax. While each of these taxes is not a huge amount by itself, there may be many such taxes, which can add up. Evidence of the tax is in the form of stamps (like postage stamps) that are affixed to the deed. The escrow company obtains the tax stamps and handles placing them on the deed for you. All that you're usually required to do is to pay the tax.

What is a *title examination fee?*

☐

As separate from a title search fee, discussed above, this is a fee for having an expert, usually an attorney, take a look at the title to the property and come up with an analysis. This is usually done only when there is a title problem, such as a lien or encumbrance, that threatens to prevent the seller from being able to complete the sale. The attorney may be able to suggest solutions to the problem. Of course, there is a fee, and you (and/or the seller) will be charged. Be sure that you're charged only if you've agreed to the examination and that the fee isn't marked up from what you agreed to pay.

What is a *title insurance fee?*

☐

Title insurance insures you against defects in the title. Public records affecting the title to the property you're buying could be incomplete or even erroneous. There could be forgeries on previous deeds. There could be legal problems with documents involved in the deeds. Title insurance offers you protection against many recorded and unrecorded problems that could adversely affect the title to the property you are buying, depending on the type of policy that you buy. Most people simply buy the cheapest policy available, and that's usually enough to protect their title against most common hazards. Note, however, as explained earlier, lenders often will require a more comprehensive (ALTA) policy that will cover them against additional risks.

What is a *wire remittance fee?*

☐

Today, most large transfers of funds are handled electronically. For example, when the escrow company sends a demand to your lender for the loan funds in order to close escrow, the lender usually sends the funds electronically. Coming from older technology when such transfers were routed to a telegraph company, these have become known as *wire transfers*. Today, they are handled mostly over the Internet through secure sites. Your escrow company may charge you a fee for handling this transfer. If the fee is small, it's probably not worth arguing about. If it's large, however, it could be nothing more than garbage. Remember, you yourself can establish "wire connections" with almost any bank and handle "wire transfers" over the Internet for free. Why should it cost the escrow company anything? Why should it involve anything more than the normal and usual process of handling an escrow?

What are *notary fees*?

It is critical to a real estate transaction that the people signing the documents are, in fact, who they say they are. For example, you want the seller to sign the deed. It won't do to have his or her brother-in-law whose name is not on the deed sign it over to you. That won't carry much weight later on when the true seller protests. The method of acknowledging the signature on a deed, or your signature on the loan agreement, is to have you sign before a notary public. This is a person who is licensed by the state (and someone who is typically independent of the transaction) to verify the authenticity of such signatures. You must present yourself, offer proof of who you are (typically a driver's license and sometimes additional documentation), and often offer a thumbprint in addition to your signature. The notary then stamps the document and signs and dates it. This makes it "official" so that it can be recorded. In most states only documents that have been notarized can be recorded. Of course, for doing this, the notary public will charge a fee. In years past this fee was nominal, perhaps only $10. Today, however, with stricter licensing and in some cases with errors and omissions (E&O) insurance policies notaries are required to have, the fees can be hefty, sometimes $25 or more per signature. While this may be included in the overall price of the escrow, it is not uncommon for escrow officers, who are also notaries, to demand a separate and additional fee. Because of the nature of the service, and assuming the fee isn't exorbitant, I would simply pay it and consider it another cost of closing the deal.

4
Attorneys' Closing Costs

QUESTIONS TO ASK YOURSELF

Why should I pay attorneys' fees?

☐

Whether to use an attorney to help in closing a common residential real estate transaction is in itself largely a matter of custom. On the West Coast and for much of the country, attorneys are seldom used as a matter of course although they are called upon in some situations if there are complex legal issues to be dealt with. On the East Coast and particularly in New York, on the other hand, it is not uncommon to have an attorney handle much of the closing including the escrow work. Chances are you'll follow custom in your area and the advice of your real estate agent. If you do use an attorney, however, you can expect his or her fee to show up on the closing statement. To be safe, you should always use an attorney in real estate transactions.

How much should I expect to pay?

☐

Attorney fees vary widely. However, on the East Coast, where attorneys regularly help with the closing of residential real estate transactions, their fees are usually between $500 and $1500, depending on the complexity of the deal and the reputation of the attorney. Since this fee includes all of the closing work, most attorneys consider it the biggest bargain in the field. On the West Coast, attorneys usually charge on an hourly basis, and again the final amount depends on the complexity of the legal matter and the reputation of the attorney. Fees of $50 to

$100 an hour are not uncommon, and fees of $200 or $300 an hour for complex tax issues are not unheard of. You should try to negotiate in advance a fee from the attorney for all of the work to be performed. It could save you money.

How do I find an attorney?

On the East Coast where they are commonly used, you'll have no problem locating one. Your agent may suggest several to choose from. Also, title insurance companies may make recommendations as will local bar associations, and in some areas attorneys advertise their services. In contrast, on the West Coast, finding an attorney who specializes in real estate transactions is like looking for a needle in a haystack. Since they aren't regularly used, there simply aren't very many of them available. However, most escrow and title insurance companies have a lawyer on call to handle legal questions, and they may make their attorneys available to you. Similarly, most large real estate offices can direct you to an attorney. My own suggestion, however, is to be wary of general-service attorneys who do not handle real estate transactions on a regular basis. It's sort of like using a general surgeon to handle a liver transplant. They simply may not be up on the finer points of closing the deal and could cause more harm than good.

QUESTIONS TO ASK YOUR ATTORNEY

Will you charge a flat fee for services?

If the attorney is going to be doing a lot of work for the closing, probably you would want a flat fee. The fee would be set up ahead of time, and after that, you wouldn't have to worry about being nickel-and-dimed with lots of small charges. Nevertheless, you want to be sure that the flat fee, indeed, is not exorbitant for the work that is to be performed. Many people do not believe that they can negotiate price with an attorney. They think that clients must simply pay the fee that is asked. In fact, you can negotiate a fee with anyone, including lawyers. It's simply a matter of bringing it up at the initial meeting (which should be a free consultation to assess your legal needs). If you can't agree on price, you can always go elsewhere.

Will you charge a document preparation fee? □

As noted above, many attorneys will simply charge a flat fee for all closing services. Some, however, break down their services. One of the inclusive fees they may charge for is document preparation. Since in a typical purchase there are relatively few documents, outside of the mortgage, for you as a buyer to sign (unless your deal requires something special), this should be a relatively small fee. (Presumably, it covers all of the paper work that the attorney prepares for you.) On the other hand, if your attorney was hired to prepare specific documentation, such as a second mortgage or a partnership agreement, then the paperwork may be more complex and the fee higher. Beware of paying for *both* an hourly wage for the attorney *and* a fee for document preparation.

Will you charge a closing documents check fee? □

One potential problem area that is frequently overlooked by buyers is the closing documents package. It is here that the escrow holder lays out all of the fees you are being charged and the lender presents you with dozens, sometimes hundreds, of pages to sign. Most buyers who infrequently purchase real estate are at a loss to understand these forms. A competent real estate attorney, on the other hand, who handles them day in and day out can perform an invaluable service for you by checking through the forms both for errors as well as for exorbitant fees and for documents that you should not sign without modification. (The attorney should be able to handle the modifications.) The attorney's fee here can be a bargain if he or she comes up with a way to avoid something that's unnecessarily costing you money or that could end up producing legal entanglements. Again, be sure you understand the attorney's fee structure and that you pay only for services actually performed.

Will you charge an escrow fee?

This is the charge that the attorney is making for running the escrow for you. As noted earlier, according to custom, depending on where you live, the attorney may or may not have an active role in handling the escrow. If he or she does, then you can expect to be charged a fee for it. You can expect that most attorneys who do run the escrow will have set up a flat fee that they will disclose when you first hire them. Of course, as with other services, you should shop around for the best deal.

What are your express letter fees?

In order to close your escrow, it may be necessary for your attorney to send (or receive) documents to people living elsewhere. This may be simpler than having them come all the way to his or her office to sign. The documents are typically sent via Federal Express, UPS Blue or Red Label, DHL, or some similar service. The fees for these services are typically around $15 or $20 per letter; however, for companies who send letters on a regular basis the express charges are deeply discounted. In my experience, attorneys tend to send all documents in this fashion. One reason is that the sender receives from the recipient, via the courier service, a signed notice specifying the date and time the package was delivered and a signature from the person who received it. Another reason that attorneys prefer the couriers is that their service is almost always faster than common postal mail. You can expect a fairly hefty express letter fee if your attorney breaks his or her closing costs down. However, you should pay only by the letter, and if it's more than $25 each, you may want to question it.

What is a *home owner's documents check fee?*

As with closing documents, home owner documents are another area where expert evaluation is, if not a necessity, then certainly highly desirable. If you're purchasing a common ownership type of property (condominium, townhouse, co-op), there will be all sorts of documents for you to look at including: conditions, covenants, and restrictions

(CCRs), bylaws, rules, lawsuits pending, home owners' organizing documents, and so on. As noted in Chapter 2, you will very likely receive a packet of all of these. But then, what do you do with that packet? Unless you are very knowledgeable in the field, you may easily miss a problem or find fault with something that's actually normal. A good attorney can quickly go over these documents and give you an opinion. Unless there's a big problem, it shouldn't take the attorney more than an hour or two to review the documents. The home owners' document check fee is the fee that the attorney charges for looking them over. Usually it's based on an hourly rate, or it is covered in the flat rate being charge for the whole closing.

What is an *attorney's inspection fee?*

You may actually want your attorney to go out to the property to take a look at a problem area. For example, there may be a dispute over a chandelier, often an area of contention. The sellers may be planning to remove it, saying it's an heirloom and they feel it's their personal property. You, on the other hand, may feel that since it was there when you looked at the property, it should be included with the sale. You need an expert to take a look at the chandelier and give you an opinion. That person will check to see how it was affixed, where it's located, take pictures of it, and so on. And it may turn out that your attorney is best suited to do this. If he or she, or more likely an assistant, goes out to the property, expect a bill for this service. Some attorneys charge their regular hourly fee, but others charge a flat fee for such services. This is almost always over and above any flat fee you may have initially negotiated for the closing.

What is an *attorney's negotiation fee?*

While in real estate it's usually agents or principals who negotiate the terms of the purchase, on some occasions you may want an attorney to handle negotiations for you. This is particularly the case when there is a complex legal question involved. For example, there may be a cloud on the title resulting from a long-forgotten lien on the property. Or there may be a boundary dispute. Or some other matter may make the property far less marketable than it other-

wise would be. You may still want to buy, but because of
the risk involved in purchasing with a defective title, you
want a significantly lower price. You may want to bring
your attorney along to explain to the seller exactly why
you think the property is worth less than he or she is asking. An attorney in this situation can prove to be invaluable
in establishing the discount you should get. In other cases,
particularly if you're buying directly from a corporation or
some other large entity, you may want an attorney to be
your representative. This charge then is the attorney's fee
for handling the negotiation. Expect it to be calculated on
an hourly basis at the highest rate. It will not usually be
included in any flat rate you initially negotiated.

Why is there a notary fee?

If your attorney is a notary public (or has one in his or her
office), expect to pay a fee for the notary services rendered for the closing. While this may be included in the
overall flat fee, it most likely won't be and will be added
on as an extra. It shouldn't be more than around $25 per
document notarized.

What is the fee for prorations?

Real estate taxes and sometimes insurance (if you take
over the seller's insurance policy) and sometimes interest are prorated. This means that, based on the closing
date, normally the sellers owe property taxes (insurance
premium and interest) for that period of time that they
owned the property. You owe for the time you will own
the property. Thus, depending on the date when you
buy and when the bills were actually paid, the sellers
may owe you money for taxes (insurance premium and
interest) that were due but not yet paid. Or you may
owe it to them for bills that they paid but that were not
yet due. The difference is paid out to whoever owes
based on a per-day ownership of the property. Normally
it is the escrow holder who calculates the prorations. If
your attorney is the person doing this, then he or she
will either charge you a separate fee or (and more likely)
he or she will include it in the flat fee for handling the
closing.

What is a *title abstract check fee?*

The abstract of title is a summary of all the changes in the title that have occurred, usually from the last time title insurance was issued, or in some cases if desired, all the way back to the first title to the property. (That can be something like a Spanish land grant or a grant of ownership from King George.) For whatever period of time it covers, the records are searched for any new liens or other encumbrances placed on the property. (An *encumbrance* is anything that gives someone other than the primary owner a secondary ownership interest in a piece of property.) There could be judgments, name disputes, boundary disputes, fraudulent signatures, or anything else. When you open an escrow account, one of the first things that the escrow holder does is order an abstract of title. It usually arrives within a week or so, and it is given to you to examine. While problems are usually noted, it is nevertheless up to you to check out the abstract and approve it in order for the closing to proceed. Unless you are familiar with real estate transactions and know what to look for, or unless the title is very clean, you should get a professional opinion on it, and an attorney can provide this opinion. However, there is usually a fee for the service. If you've negotiated a flat rate for the attorney's fees, checking the title abstract is normally included in that fee. Otherwise, your attorney may charge you for an hour or so of his or her time.

What is a *consulting fee?*

You've hired your attorney as a consultant. However, he or she may not know all the answers. Indeed, attorneys may need to consult someone else on occasion. This is often the case in arcane matters such as unusual tax situations. The consulting fee covers the charges for the consultant's services. It is almost never included in the flat fee you may have initially negotiated. If it's expert legal services, expect the fee to be very high. If it's the services of a CPA or other professional accountant, it will probably not be as steep. Usually the fee is assessed on an hourly basis, and it covers researching the problem and coming up with a solution.

2

Closing the Offer

5
Negotiating the Closing Costs

QUESTIONS TO ASK YOURSELF

Can I have someone else pay my closing costs?

Yes, you can. Anyone can pay your closing costs, if someone is willing to do so. However, there are certain restrictions on this practice, most noticeably coming from the lender. If you're financing the purchase, most lenders will want to see that you come up at least with the *recurring closing costs.* These are such things as interest, your share of taxes, and insurance. Most lenders feel that if you can't handle these expenses, you may not be able to handle the financing, and they could consequently refuse to fund the mortgage. Another factor is who gets the tax write-off for those closing costs that are tax deductible (such as some points). If you don't pay them, you're probably not entitled to get the deduction. If someone else pays them who doesn't have his or her name on the title to the property, he or she may not be entitled to a write-off either. Check with your accountant.

Who else would pay my closing costs?

The two most likely candidates are the seller and the lender. Of course, there's always the exceptional situation in which a family member or close friend might be willing to give you a gift or a loan to cover the closing costs.

When can I negotiate the closing costs with the seller?

The time to negotiate having the seller pay your closing costs is when you are making your offer to purchase. The only way you'll normally be able to get a seller, for example, to cover your closing costs is to make it a condition of the sale. You put it this way: "Mr. Seller, if you want me to buy your home, you're going to have to pay some of my closing costs. If you don't pay them, I'll move on and not purchase your property." This transaction is handled by including a contingency clause in the purchase agreement. It essentially says that your purchase is "subject to" the seller's paying all or a specific amount of your closing costs. In a hot real estate market when properties are selling quickly, no sane seller would accept such terms, and your offer will be rejected. However, in a very slow market when the seller hasn't had an offer in 6 months, your terms of having him or her pay the closing costs might very well be accepted. It's important to understand, however, that if you make your purchase contingent on the seller's paying the closing costs and the seller refuses, you won't get the house without paying the closing costs yourself. Making this offer involves a certain amount of risk that you could lose the property.

When should I negotiate the closing costs with the lender?

This negotiation should be made at the time you apply for your mortgage, which should be after you've got a signed purchase agreement. (This is not to be confused with mortgage preapproval, which you should obtain as soon as you start looking—it gets a lender to commit to giving you a mortgage based on your income, cash, and credit.) The questions to ask the lender are noted below. Keep in mind, however, that if you want to roll the closing costs into a higher price, you must do so as part of the negotiating process with the seller. Beware of having a purchase agreement that shows an initial low negotiating price without the seller's paying your closing costs, then goes UP to a higher price with the seller's paying your closing costs. The lender will probably balk at this. Most lenders do not want to finance the closing costs as part of a higher mortgage without doing it directly themselves.

Do I have the cash to pay the closing costs?

To paraphrase the poet Robert Frost, sometimes the best way around a problem is through it. If you have the cash to pay your closing costs, you may be better off doing that. The reason is that it makes for a clean deal, without any complications. You are more likely to get a better price from the seller and a better loan from the lender in a clean deal. On the other hand, if cash is a problem for you, then one way to reduce the amount of cash you'll need to close the deal is to have someone else pay your closing costs for you.

QUESTIONS TO ASK THE SELLER

Will you accept a deal with your paying my NRCCs?

The most common way to structure a transaction in which you ask the seller to pay your NRCCs is this: You write it as a condition of sale in your purchase agreement. The most common way of handling this is to ask the seller to pay your nonrecurring closing costs (NRCCs). These costs can be substantial and can include all of the following:

- Your portion of the title insurance charge
- Your portion of the escrow charge
- Some of your points on the loan
- Your attorney's fees
- Your appraisal fee
- Your portion (if any) of the termite and/or fungus clearance charges
- Any other one-time fees that you would otherwise pay as part of the closing

Frequently the NRCCs can be many thousands of dollars, money that would otherwise come out of your pocket. Remember, the seller risks losing the deal by not paying your NRCCs. In a hot market where properties are selling quickly, some sellers won't even bother to counteroffer. They'll simply reject your offer out of hand. However, in a tight market where the seller is eager to sell and doesn't have any other buyers, it can be a different story.

Will you pay all of my closing costs to make the deal?

Here, in addition to the NRCCs you've asked the seller to pay, you're also asking that he or she pay the following:

- Any interest on your new loan that you owe in closing whether it be in the form of points or prorations
- The buyer's share of tax prorations
- The buyer's hazard insurance policy
- Any and all other closing costs that the buyer has

There is no law against the seller's picking up *all* of your closing costs, and some desperate sellers will indeed do this. However, don't expect to get the seller to agree to *both* pick up your closing costs *and* give you a good deal on the price unless the market is really slow. Also, note that many lenders will not give you financing when the seller is picking up *all* of your closing costs.

Will you accept a higher price in exchange for paying my closing costs?

This is very tricky. Here you are saying to the seller, "If you are willing to pay my NRCCs (or *all* of my closing costs), I will give you a higher price to compensate." In practice, this means that if your closing costs are $5000 and the price is $200,000, you'll pay the seller $205,000, which is $5000 more for the property and he or she will pay your closing costs. Since almost all of that money comes in the form of a new higher mortgage, many sellers are agreeable, even in a tight market. (It's simply no skin off their nose.) On the other hand, if the lender sees what you are doing, it may object. It may feel that you are artificially inflating the price of the property and the financing. The answer here is to have a solid appraisal showing that the value of the property is no higher than the total price you are paying. (The lender won't give you a loan based on a price higher than appraisal anyhow.) Many real estate agents who have been in the business for a long time will simply write up a clean contract showing the final price and terms and not showing the negotiation that went on beforehand in order to make it a clean deal. If you qualify and if the property is appraised by the lender at the price you want, there's probably no logical reason not to offer you full financing.

Will you accept a second mortgage for my closing costs?

Another method is to borrow your closing costs from the seller. Typically sellers receive lots of cash when they sell their property. But they may not want cash. This is often the case if they are retired and are not rolling the money over into another, bigger house. What they may want is interest income. You can offer that to them at a rate far higher than they are likely to get at the bank. You simply offer to give them a second mortgage for your NRCCs (or *all* of your closing costs). They use some of the cash coming from the sale to pay your closing costs. And you give them a second mortgage for that amount. If bank interest rates are paying 2 percent and you give them a 7 percent second, they may be very interested. Keep in mind, however, that the second mortgage will have to be paid back. You're only *borrowing* the money. However, you can structure the payback to most conveniently suit you. For example, you can pay it back over 5 or 10 years, principal and interest. Or to reduce your payments, you may want to pay back interest only, with a balloon for the principal at the end. Or to really reduce your payment you may want to pay it back in a lump sum at the time you resell your property. This way while interest accrues, it and the principal are not paid until you resell at sometime in the future—you have *no* monthly payments! Be aware, however, that many lenders today are looking at the combined loan to value (CLTV) ratio. This means that they may want you to qualify not only for their own first mortgage but for the combined first and second mortgages! If you're borderline on income or credit, this could be a problem.

QUESTIONS TO ASK THE LENDER

Can my closing costs be added to the mortgage?

In years past this was a no-no. Lenders never wanted to roll your closing costs into a higher mortgage. Today, however, with greater competition and with more rationality in the lending field, many lenders are more than willing to go along. Many lenders will lend a mortgage based on the maximum appraised value of the property (assuming, of course, you qualify). If that includes money that is used to pay for your NRCCs, they will go along. Some may balk, however, if you try to get it to cover *all* of your closing costs. In that case, you'll simply have to look for a more lenient lender. Be very wary, however, of going for a mortgage for *more* than the appraised value. Today some lenders will offer highly qualified buyers a mortgage of up to 125 percent of valuation. This could get you into the property. But if something unexpected and adverse happens (such as losing your job, getting sick, or getting a divorce), you probably won't be able to immediately sell the property and get out of the financing because you'll owe more than it's worth. This means you could lose the property (and your credit) in foreclosure. Never try to get a higher loan by having the appraiser overstate the value of the property. Ultimately this usually results in the appraiser, the lender, and you getting in serious trouble with the federal government. Coercing or paying off an appraiser to get a better evaluation brings with it severe penalties.

Can my closing costs be traded for a higher interest rate?

This is the most common way of financing closing costs today. It is routinely done with *no-cost re-fis*. As a home buyer, you can probably find a lender willing to do it for you. Here's how it works: If the market rate for the mortgage is, for example, 6 percent and your closing costs are $3000, the lender may be willing to pay your NRCCs *if* you are willing to accept a mortgage of 6⅜ percent. You give the lender more interest, and it pays your closing costs. The amount of the loan remains the same. However, your monthly payments are slightly higher to reflect the higher interest rate. Of course, this works only if you have enough income and strong enough credit to qualify under a slightly higher interest rate. Keep in mind, that even here, the lenders are unlikely to pay *all* of your closing costs. You'll still have to come up with those that recur.

Can my closing costs be financed through a second mortgage?

You may be able to cut a deal with a lender for a second mortgage to cover your closing costs. Here, instead of the seller's coming up with the cash, the money is coming from the lender. This can be the same lender from whom you are getting your new first mortgage, or it can be a separate lender. What it amounts to is a new mortgage, a second, on the property. The lender gives you the cash to pay the closing costs—you give the lender the loan. However, as opposed to getting a second from a seller, here you will not be able to dictate the terms. The lender will tell you what the interest rate will be. (It's usually slightly higher than that for a first mortgage.) The lender will also tell you the term offered (typically from 3 to 15 years) and the monthly payment. Nevertheless, if you are cash poor and need to close, this is one method that should work.

Can I charge my closing costs to my credit card(s)?

Of course, you can. However, doing so will amount to taking a cash advance on which you usually would have to start repaying at a very high interest rate immediately. I would suggest you do this only as a last alternative and have a backup plan (such as refinancing the property or getting a second mortgage on it) for paying off the high-interest-rate credit.

Will you cut my closing costs in exchange for my using your firm to finance my purchase?

Here you're trying to negotiate with a lender to give you a better deal (lower interest rate, higher mortgage, closing costs rolled in, and so on) in exchange for your business. While the tendency is to brush this off as an impossible dream, don't. Particularly if you're dealing with a mortgage broker, who usually gets paid only if and when you get the financing. You may have some surprising stretch room. Particularly if the refinancing market isn't too hot (not too many people are refinancing their home mortgages), the mortgage broker may be able to find a lender who's more amenable to your wishes. The mortgage broker may even be willing to throw in some of his or her fee to make it all happen. This is a situation in which you'll never know unless you ask.

6
Creating a Powerful Purchase Agreement

QUESTIONS TO ASK YOURSELF

How does the purchase agreement affect the closing?

The purchase agreement is the governing document of the transaction. Not only does it specify the price you'll pay for the property, it also gives the terms. Indeed, *closing* usually means completing the terms of the purchase agreement.

Was the purchase agreement written by a licensed and experienced agent?

The purchase agreement is the lead document that defines the transaction. Besides the price and the amount of the deposit, it also indicates whether or not you'll get financing (and what kind) as well as any other terms and conditions of the deal. It should even mention any personal property, such as a chandelier, that might be included. Anything that's left out won't be part of the deal. To be effective, the agreement must be signed both by you and by the seller, meaning that it has to accurately reflect the seller's desires as well as yours. For that reason, it is difficult to write a purchase agreement that reflects everyone's concerns. Usually a competent and experienced real estate agent (or attorney) is the best person to handle it.

Did an attorney check the document?

The purchase agreement is intended to be a legally binding document. Once you sign it, presumably you're on
the hook for what it says. If you aren't properly protected
by the language of the document, you might not get the
property. Indeed, it might cost you money. It could even
result in your becoming involved in a lawsuit. Therefore,
it's important that the document be properly drawn, and
the best way to be sure that it has been is to have it examined by a competent attorney. In an effort to avoid legal
entanglements, today's purchase agreements are typically 5 to 10 pages long and are filled with boilerplate
legalese. Often most of the terms are agreed to simply by
checking a box. Nevertheless, the devil is in the details,
and you want to be assured that the boilerplate language
is appropriate and that the right boxes have been
checked. Have an attorney look it over. The few bucks it
costs will be well worth it.

Is the property address correct?

It's surprising that more people don't buy the wrong
house because of an incorrectly written address. It's easy
to write the wrong address. And always remember that
the address tacked onto the outside of the house could be
inaccurate. The address 2124 Maple Street might actually
be 2421 Maple Street. While a wrong address can easily be
corrected later in the transaction as long as both the buyer
and the seller want the deal to move forward, a seller who
wants to back out can use an incorrectly written address
as a wedge to scuttle the deal. Further, remember that the
street address is not the legal address of the property—it
is only a convenient designation used for mail delivery,
fire protection, and other similar purposes. The legal address is a description such as "lot 41, map 24, of the Smith
subdivision recorded in book 29 of the city of Maple-
ville." In fact, as soon as you open an escrow account, a
title search normally will be conducted, and part of the
reason it is accomplished at the very beginning of the
closing procedures is to verify the legal address. You
should be shown the address and asked to corroborate its
accuracy. Your agent and attorney can help you here. Just

to be sure that the address doesn't present a problem, many agents will identify the property by its legal address (if they know it) or next best (if they don't) by referring to the property as "commonly known as 2124 Maple Street."

Am I putting up a sufficient deposit?

Your deposit is technically called *earnest money*. Its purpose is to show that your intent to purchase the property is sincere—in other words, that you are acting in earnest. Presumably, the amount that you put up should reflect just how earnest you actually are. The larger the deposit, the more sincere you are presumed to be in making the purchase. The smaller the deposit, the less determined. Ideally, you want to put up a deposit big enough to impress the seller with your sincerity in making the purchase but small enough so that if for some reason you lose the deposit, you won't be severely hurt financially. That's the theory. In today's market, however, with buyers having weeks to remove inspection contingencies, give approval to the seller's disclosures, and get financing, the initial deposit isn't nearly as important. After all, the seller knows you probably have many ways of getting out of the deal, at least initially, without the penalty of a lost deposit. Therefore, a smaller initial deposit may be just as acceptable as a larger one.

Why does the purchase agreement call for an increase in my deposit?

Some contracts that offer an initially small deposit call for a hefty increase in the deposit amount after the usual contingencies (inspection, disclosure, and financing) have been removed. The reason is that at this point, if you refuse to go through with the purchase, the seller may indeed be entitled to keep your deposit. The deposit amount, therefore, now carries far more weight. The seller is asking you to now increase your deposit to prove your sincerity in intending to complete the transaction. By complying, you will show you are in earnest because you will have far more to lose if you don't follow through with the deal. If you harbor any hopes of backing out of the deal, increasing your deposit is not something you want to do. If you're not clear on your situation, be sure to have your attorney explain the consequences of backing out of the deal.

To whom is my deposit check written?

Usually most agents will ask that you write your deposit check payable to an escrow company. Thus, the only entity that can cash it is the escrow holder. The money is immediately deposited, and there it will stay until both you and the sellers (or a court) agree how it will be dispersed. Technically, the deposit is the property of the sellers, and they can demand that you write out the check to them. However, if you do so, you put yourself at risk. The sellers can cash the check, and then, later on, if the deal doesn't go through and you are entitled to receive your deposit back, they may be unwilling or unable to pay you. Writing the deposit check to the sellers' agent may be equally as dangerous since the agent is responsible to the sellers, and if the sellers demand that the agent fork over the money, he or she may be obligated to do so.

Does the deposit specify that it is to go toward the purchase price?

The rationale underlying this requirement is so simple that sometimes the requirement is overlooked, with what can be dire consequences for you, the buyer. Yes, the deposit shows that you're sincere. But once the deal is concluded, you want that deposit to be part of your down payment, part of the purchase price. However, unless the purchase document specifically says that the deposit must be applied to the purchase price, it might be interpreted that the deposit is *in addition* to the purchase price. Thus you'd have to pay your down payment and get your financing on top of the deposit you gave. Handling the deposit this way would increase the cost of the house. This sort of problem rarely happens, but it doesn't hurt to verify that the deposit is to be part of the purchase price.

Are the loan amount, rate, term, and type correct?

Of all home purchases made, 90 percent involve financing of one sort or another. However, it's not enough to simply state that you're going to get a mortgage. In order to protect you, the contract needs to specify exactly what kind of mortgage, and for how much. After all, anyone can get some sort of a mortgage, even though the interest rate may not be low enough or the payments may not be low enough to make it affordable. Can't get the amount specified, the interest rate, the points, the term (length of mortgage, for example, 30 years), or type (fixed rate or some type of adjustable rate)? Then if the contract is properly drawn with a typical finance contingency, you should *not* be obligated to complete the transaction.

Why does the purchase agreement have a mortgage interest rate that is higher than the current market rate?

It's important to understand that the mortgage market is constantly in flux. Rates are always in motion moving up or down depending on the demand for mortgage money, the overall health of the economy, the availability of funds, and other factors. Thus, while the current rate when you make your purchase offer may be 7 percent, for example, by the time you close, it could be 8 or 6 percent. Thus, if your contract specified that you will get a mortgage at 7 percent, and the market shifted even slightly higher, you wouldn't be locked into completing the deal. And as a result, the sellers might not be willing to sign the contract. Thus, in order to lock you in and appease the sellers' concerns, contracts often will specify a mortgage rate that's slightly higher than the current market rate. For example, when the market is 7 percent, the contract may specify that you'll get a mortgage interest rate for not more than 7.5 or even 8 percent.

Is the interest rate low enough to protect me?

While 1 or 2 percent more than the prevailing market rate may not seem like a lot, in reality it can have a big effect on your monthly payments. For example, for a $200,000 mortgage written for 30 years, the difference in the monthly payment between a 7 percent loan and an 8 percent loan is about $140 a month. The interest rate goes up a mere 1 percent, and suddenly your monthly payment jumps up $140 more. That's probably okay for many people, but if you're scrimping just trying to get into the home, the affordability issue for you could be huge. That extra $140 might mean the difference between being able to make the monthly payments and not. You want to be sure that while the purchase agreement includes enough flexibility to satisfy the seller that you're locked in (see the previous question), it also offers enough protection to you so that you won't get yourself into a situation that you can't afford. You may want to insist, for example, that the maximum interest rate be at market or only a quarter point or a half point above, rather than a full point. You can expect both the seller and your agent to fight you on this because the closer you get to the interest rate at market, the less locked into the deal you are.

Is there a contingency letting me out if I can't get the financing?

A *contingency* is a clause that says something is subject to something else. For example, your purchase may be subject to your getting financing at the terms specified (see the above two questions). If you don't get the financing you've specified, then you're out of the contract—you don't have to buy the property, and you get your deposit back. (Of course, you could always opt to continue with the purchase, but the option would be yours.) Most purchase agreements contain a financing contingency similar to one just described in order to protect the buyer. After all, if you can't get your financing, then presumably you can't afford to buy the home and should be let out of the deal. Be wary if your contract does not contain a financing contingency (see the next question).

What happens if I waive the financing contingency?

In recent years with very hot markets and competing offers on homes, some buyers, in order to sweeten the pot, have removed the financing contingency. Thus, they are saying to the seller, "I will purchase this home even if I can't get financing. In other words, I'm in effect offering a cash deal to you." (Of course, the buyer still may hope to go out and get financing.) To a seller, these words are golden since they mean that if the buyer doesn't go through with the purchase even though no loan is available, that seller gets to keep the deposit. (Presumably the buyer includes a larger deposit to show sincerity.) However, from a buyer's perspective, this is obviously a most dangerous course to take. Some buyers who have solid preapproval from a lender and/or have other sources of funds may use it as a technique to win the bidding in a multiple-offer situation. However, if anything goes wrong and the buyer can't get sufficient funds to make the deal, the deposit could be lost. And worse, the seller could sue for specific performance. Removing the financing contingency is not to be taken lightly. If you want to do it, be sure you first check with your attorney for the potential consequences.

Is there enough time allowed for me to get financing?

Time is the essence of real estate transactions. They are not open ended, meaning that the deals won't wait forever. Normally a limited amount of time is given, after the purchase agreement is signed, for you to get financing. If you don't or can't get financing within that time limit, then the sellers may be within their rights to back out of the deal. Chances are you'll get your deposit back, but you won't get the house. Therefore, it's very important that there be enough time allowed for you to get your financing. How much time is enough? If you've already gone to a reputable lender and that lender has preapproved you, meaning that they've checked your credit, assets, and income and it has given you a letter telling you how much it will lend, then the time could be very short, perhaps as little as a week or less. On the other hand, if you have to now start your search for a lender and get approval (including removing or explaining away any bad reports on your credit), it could take anywhere from 3 to 6 weeks or longer. Typically most sellers in today's market are not willing to wait much longer than a month. Some insist on closing within 2 to 3 weeks. Therefore, it behooves you to get preapproval *before* making your purchase offer.

Is the time for acceptance of the offer short?

Every purchase agreement should have written into it the amount of time you give the sellers to accept your offer. For example, you might give them a week, or a day, or an hour. If they haven't accepted your offer exactly as you've presented it within the time limit, then your offer is with-drawn. As a practical matter, it's usually a good idea to give the sellers a very short time to accept, typically 1 day or less. While this may seem counterintuitive, since you want the sellers to have time to seriously consider what you're proposing, it's actually a very strategic move. Giving the sellers a short time to accept helps to prevent other offers from coming in and beating yours. (All offers are supposed to be presented as they are made and not wait in line until preceding offers are accepted or rejected.) Also, it forces the sellers to take action one way or another. They must decide to accept or reject (or counter) your offer. Give them enough time, and they just might sit on the fence and never make a decision. A good rule of thumb is to make the time for acceptance reasonable, but short.

Will I get possession at the close of escrow?

The purchase agreement should specify *when* you'll get possession of the home. Usually, the transfer of the property from the sellers to the buyer takes place at the close of escrow when the deal normally ends, but not always. For example, you may want to move in sooner because of commitments at work, or because of your children's school starting date. If the deal looks solid, you may be able to work out moving in a few days or weeks early with the sellers. They will probably want you to sign a rental agreement and perhaps put up a (sometimes hefty) security deposit. Sometimes repair work may be required as part of the transaction, and it won't be done by the time escrow closes. In that case, you might still close and get possession a few days later, although for financial safety you may want to delay closing the escrow, if possible, until all repair work is completed and you can be given possession. (See also Chapter 6.)

Do the sellers want a rent-back clause?

Sometimes the sellers don't want to give you possession of the property when escrow closes. (See the previous question.) Rather, they have their own reasons for staying on for a time. For example, they don't want to move their children out of their local schools until the term is up, or they have a few more months of employment in the area, or they have not yet closed on a new home they are buying. As a result, the purchase agreement may specify that the sellers are to keep possession of the property for a stated period of time. Usually there is a corresponding statement that they agree to pay rent, typically at least equal to your monthly payments, during their possession. If this occurs, remember, after the close of escrow, the sellers convert to being tenants with all the rights tenants have in your state. That means that if they don't move as agreed, you'll have to go through the hassle of a court eviction (unlawful detainer action). To help put you on firmer ground, have the sellers sign a separate, tight rental agreement. (You'll want your agent or attorney to draw this up.) Be sure that they also agree to put up a hefty security and cleaning deposit. And conduct a credit check on them. (In a purchase, everyone wants to know about your credit, but no one asks about the sellers' credit!) If the sellers don't have good credit, you may want to rethink giving them possession after the escrow closing. In fact, if there's any way to avoid it and still make the deal, you are usually better off refusing to let the sellers retain possession after the close of escrow.

Is all personal property listed?

There is probably no area of purchasing a home that leads to more conflict than personal property. It's important to know what it is. The land and anything *appurtenant* (attached) to it is considered real estate. *Everything else* is personal property. That means that while the windows in your home are real estate, the shades and drapes are probably personal property. While the countertop is real property, a countertop stove that just unplugs is probably personal property! Throw-rugs, furniture, even chandeliers that easily detach are probably considered personal property. Therefore, it is to your advantage to have listed in the purchase agreement as part of the real property all items that might be confused for personal property. A good real estate agent will automatically include a paragraph that says that all wall and floor coverings (carpets, drapes, shades, and so on) are considered part of the real estate. The agent will also list all appliances including stoves, ovens, dishwashers, refrigerators, and washers and dryers that go with the sale and that might be otherwise considered personal property. And finally, added to the list should be those items that might cause confusion such as a fancy chandelier, a bird feeder, a barbecue, a work bench, or removable shelves. You have to assume that if it's not on the list as included with the real estate, it's probably personal property and the sellers can take it with them. Don't get into a squabble after the deal has closed because you forgot to list some item important to you as part of the real property.

Is there a disclosure contingency?

Most, but not all, states require the sellers to give you full disclosure of any known defects in the property. You want to be sure that either your state real estate code provides for such disclosure (check with a good real estate agent), or if not your purchase agreement specifies that the sellers must provide you with full disclosure and that your purchase is contingent upon your approving their disclosures. There are two reasons you want disclosures. First, the sellers may disclose something about the property that may make you want out of the deal. The house could be on an earthquake fault. Or there could be an underground river running beneath the house. Or there could be hidden cracks in the foundation. Upon disclosure, you may realize that the pretty house you were planning to buy in reality is a rotten fixer-upper and you don't want any part of it, at least not at the price you were prepared to pay. The other reason is that when the sellers give you disclosures, they go on record as to what they know is wrong with the property. Later on after the deal has closed, if you discover a major problem that they knew about (as revealed by work receipts, obvious recent and insufficient repairs, or even neighbors' observations), you have a much stronger case for forcing them to pay to correct the problem.

Is there a home inspection contingency?

A home inspection contingency gives you the right to have a professional inspector check out the property, and it also makes the deal subject to your approval of his or her inspection report. Without it, you'd have to take the home, in a sense, sight unseen. Of course, you have to pay the inspection cost, typically $250 to $300. But at least you'll be able to gracefully get out of the deal if the inspector finds something. Many purchase agreements today come with this as an automatic part of the boilerplate, but some do not. Be sure that yours is written in such a way that not only do you have the right to bring in a professional inspector but you also have the right to approve or disapprove of the report. Just having the right to have an inspection isn't good enough. The deal must hinge on your having the right to say yea or nay to what the inspector finds. Sometimes sellers will insist that you can disapprove of the report only if the inspector finds a significant defect in the property. This weakens your position. Also, be sure the clause gives you the right to be shown all previous inspection reports on the property. And be sure you have a good agent write in (or check over) the contingency, and have your attorney look it over as well.

Does the home inspection contingency give me enough time?

It takes time to find a home inspector, to line up the inspection, and to get the report. You want to be sure your contingency clause allows you enough time. Typically this is 14 days, at minimum. There should also be an automatic extension allowed if the inspection reveals a significant defect and you need to call in specialists. For example, the professional home inspector might find a big crack in the foundation. Now you want to call in a structural engineer to check it out. This can take additional time. Keep in mind that the contingency will not usually specify who is to conduct the inspection. That's up to you. Your agent can usually suggest someone, but you'll want to be sure that the person is both a member of local trade groups as well as either the American Society of Home Inspectors (ASHI) or the National Association of Home Inspectors (NAHI) or a similar organization. (See Internet Resources at the end of this book.) Be aware that most states do *not* as of this time license home inspectors.

Do I have active or passive approval?

The method by which you are to give your approval of the home inspection report and other contingencies is often specified in the purchase agreement. If you have *passive* approval, it means that if you don't disapprove the report, usually in writing, by the specified time limit, it is assumed that you approve it. In that case the contingency is automatically removed, and the deal moves forward. If you have *active* approval, you must approve the report within the specified time, again usually in writing; otherwise, it is assumed you disapprove, and the deal can be dissolved. Be sure you know what your time limits are and how you are to respond. You can lose a deal by failing to act appropriately. If you're not certain, be sure to check with your agent and/or attorney for advice. Note that either disapproving or failing to approve is not necessarily fatal to the deal. Rather, it can open the whole process of negotiation again, in which case you can demand that the seller correct a problem or give you a price reduction to compensate for it.

Is there a termite and/or pest inspection contingency?

Most purchase agreements call for a termite report and clearance, which usually includes a pest inspection. Again this is often part of the boilerplate. The reason for the inspection is that usually no lender will give you financing until you can get a certificate showing that your home is free of termites. However, even if the lender doesn't insist on this, you should. Typically the seller will pay for the report and will pay to have the termites removed and also pay to have any existing termite damage repaired. However, usually you will be asked to pay for any preventive work to correct future infestation. Normally, you have a choice as to whether you want to have this preventive work done. If you don't have it done, you don't have to pay, and it isn't done. Since preventive work is many times problematic (there may be no proof that it will do any good), most buyers refuse to have it done. If the seller refuses to or can't produce a termite clearance, the deal collapses, and usually you're out of it.

Do I have approval of repair work?

Many times the purchase agreement will specify that if there is repair work to be done either because of the home inspection report, the termite inspection report, or other inspections, the sellers have the option of determining who will do that work. That means that they can choose to have a professional do it or a handy person, or they might even do it themselves to save money. Since a professional is usually the most expensive, oftentimes sellers will opt to handle repair work themselves, which is usually the cheapest answer. The problem is that the result may be shoddy work. For example, there may be dry rot in a bathroom floor so it needs to be replaced. A professional wants $500 to do it, but the seller decides to lay the linoleum tiles himself, which will cost only $50. However, the tiles he puts down end up being ill matched and curling up. Ideally your inspection, termite, or other contingencies will specify that you have the right to approve all work; in other words, you have the right to see that it is done as well as possible. This also usually gives you the right to insist that it be done by a professional. If you don't like the work, it has to be done over.

Does the termite report include inspection for black mold?

Black mold is the latest environmental concern of most buyers. It is mold that grows on almost anything from sheetrock to clothes and furniture. It occurs primarily in damp climates. It first came to attention in Florida and the South, and then it moved to Texas, from where concern spread nationally. The jury is out on whether it is harmful to people, although some who are exposed to it claim to have severe allergic reactions. However, finding black mold in a home could possibly lower its value in today's market. You should check to see that your termite and/or pest inspection covers looking for it. And, as with termites, any black mold that is found should be removed, and repairs should be made to the underlying material if necessary—all paid for by the seller.

Am I having a soils report?

Your professional home inspector may suggest that you have a soils report. Or if there are known soil problems in the area, your agent may write in a contingency requiring your approval of a soils report. This is typically done by an engineering firm that will analyze the soil to determine if there are problems with building on it. For example, in some areas the soil may be subject to liquefaction in earthquakes, meaning that it could move and cause the house to tumble down. In other areas it may contain too much moisture and not be able to withstand the weight of the home over time. In yet other areas there may be water seeping through it at certain times of the year, causing standing water to accumulate in the yard. A soils report will usually reveal these and other problems that you may or may not want to make an issue of.

What about a geological report?

In certain parts of the country, California, for example, the seller may be required to provide (or you may demand) a geological report. This assessment will be done by an engineering firm and will typically make references to public geological surveys. It will tell you the location of fault lines and the proximity of the property to them. It will also point out other geological hazards. There is usually nothing that can be done to remove the risks; however, you should know about them so that you can weigh them in making your decision on whether to buy the property.

Will I need a flood plain or other water report contingency?

In many parts of the country, excess water is a big concern. In the Midwest, for example, you may want to know if your property is on a flood plain. The land may be perfectly dry when you're looking at it. But it could be near a river, for example, that occasionally (annually, every 10 years, every 100 or 500 years) will overflow its banks and flood your property. Or you could be near the seashore and be subject to heavy surf and flooding during storms. This report should tell you what the risks are. It may be essential to your being able to get home owners' insurance. In some areas, insurance companies will refuse to issue insurance because of the danger of flooding, and consequently lenders may not be willing to offer you a mortgage because you cannot obtain the necessary insurance.

Is there a land survey?

While this is not as common in urban areas, a land survey contingency is an absolute necessity in many rural areas.

A land survey is made by a surveyor who examines the property to determine its actual boundaries. Typically the surveyor will put in place a series of markers to show the boundaries. The reason you need to have a survey conducted is that without the survey, you won't know what land you're buying. You can't assume that a fence running along the side of the property is necessarily on the property line. It may be inside or outside the line. Or there may be encumbrances, other homes, for example, built on the subject home's land. This can result in all sorts of nasty title problems, which you'll want the sellers to resolve before you complete the purchase. Ask your agent if you should have a survey done.

Are other reports needed?

There are as many reports available as there are conditions that may affect the property. For example, if the home uses a well instead of public water, you will want to be sure to have a report on the well—Is the water potable, what condition is it in, is there danger of contamination from nearby septic systems, and so on. While these conditions are many of those typically covered under the umbrella of a home inspection report, if any known problem exists in the area, a good agent will write them in as additional contingencies. In other words, you should have the right to approve or disapprove them.

Is there a provision for retrofitting?

In some areas retrofitting of older homes to modern standards for withstanding earthquakes or other hazards may be possible, or even be required. Check with a builder or your agent. Typically either the seller will pay for this, or the cost will be split between the buyer and the seller. Keep in mind that retrofitting can be extremely expensive, and it could be a deal breaker. The seller may refuse to pay for retrofitting, arguing that the house has survived for many years without the feature that is being considered and the house doesn't need the feature now. You must now decide whether you can live without the retrofitting, you want it and want to pay for it yourself, or you don't want to bother with retrofitting and instead want to quit the deal because of the missing feature. Be sure you get expert technical advice before you make your decision.

Are there other needed contingencies?

A contingency can be inserted about almost anything. For example, a common contingency that you as a buyer may want involves selling an existing home. You may want to insert into the contract that your purchase is subject to your ability to sell your old home. If you can't sell your old home, you aren't required to buy the new one. In a slow real estate market, sellers will often accept such contingencies. When the market is hot, however, and buyers are plentiful, sellers will usually refuse them. Be sure to express clearly to your agent what contingency requirements you have. Don't assume the agent will automatically include them. Further, think long and hard before being talked out of including a contingency. In our example, if you couldn't sell your old home and were required to go through with the purchase of the new home, you might end up with two properties and two mortgages, which you might not be able to afford. Remember that a contingency can protect you.

Are there any contingencies added by or favoring the sellers?

Sellers can add contingencies favoring them. For example, they could add a contingency that says you agree to pay their real estate commission. Or that says that you agree to pay for a home warranty plan (see below). Or almost anything else. Carefully check for any contingencies added by or favoring the sellers. You'll want your agent and attorney to check them as well.

Are the sellers providing a home warranty plan?

A *home warranty plan* is an insurance policy that provides a benefit if any of the covered home systems break down. It is usually good for a year, and the cost of it is normally born by the sellers. Home warranty plans are offered by several companies, and generally they cover such things as appliances, heating and/or air-conditioning systems, basic electrical and plumbing systems (including water heater), and so on. For an additional fee, you can sometimes also get coverage for the roof (leaks that can be fixed by repair, not usually replacement), pools, spas, and other such features. In order to qualify for the plan, the sellers must normally certify that everything in the property is in good working condition at the time of the sale. During the year if you have a problem with, for example, a dishwasher or garbage disposal, the two items most likely to cause difficulty, you can call a special number and a ser-vice person will be sent out to fix the problem. You'll have to pay a deductible that typically ranges from $35 to $50. Consequently, you have to decide up front if you think the cost of the service is going to be more or less than the deductible. Typically, assuming you haven't used your warranty plan too much, you will qualify for a renewal in your second year of ownership. (Sometimes the renewal is for a steeply sharper fee.) By then you should have a good idea if the plan is worthwhile or not.

Will I get a *final walk-through?*

A final walk-through normally occurs just a day or so before escrow is ready to close at which time the title to the property is given to you. Its purpose is to allow you to once more inspect the property, mainly to see that it's in the same shape that it was in when you made your purchase offer. The concern is that during the 30 days or so it takes to close escrow, the sellers may have allowed the property to deteriorate. They may not have kept up the watering and cleaning. Or, what's worse, they may have thrown a couple of wild parties that have resulted in damage to the property. The final walk-through is your chance to bring such problems to the sellers' attention so that the sellers can correct them before the sale is closed and you lose your leverage. It's important to understand that the purpose of the final walk-through is not to give you an opportunity to reopen negotiations or to back out of the deal. In fact, many purchase agreement *final-walk-through* clauses specifically state this. Nevertheless, in a properly drawn up clause (one that protects you), you should have the right to refuse to close until significant damage has been repaired to your satisfaction. If you're not sure that the clause in your contract protects you adequately, have your attorney check it over. (See also Chapter 15.)

Is an escrow company listed?

Sometimes either the sellers or one of the agents will insist on a particular escrow company to handle the closing. If it's the sellers who are insisting, chances are they bought the house within the past 3 years or so, and the escrow company they used then has offered them a discount on their share of the escrow fees if they return to the same company. If it's an agent, chances are the agent's company has an interest in the escrow company. Ethically, and in some cases legally, the agent should not steer you to a particular escrow company, particularly if they are getting a kick-back for doing so. If an agent insists on a particular escrow company, you may want to likewise insist that he or she state in writing that he or she is not being compensated by the escrow company named in the referral. Your insistence on this may change the agent's mind about making the referral.

Is a title insurance company listed?

Similarly, sometimes either the sellers or one of the agents will insist on a particular title insurance company to handle the closing. If it's the sellers, chances are they bought the house within the past 3 years or so and the title insurance company they worked with at that time has offered them a discount on their share of the title insurance fees if they return to the same company. If it's an agent, chances are the agent's company has an interest in the title insurance company. Ethically, and in some cases legally, the agent should not steer you to a particular title company if he or she is getting a kick-back for doing so. If an agent insists on a particular title insurance company, you may want to likewise insist that he or she state in writing that he or she is not being compensated for steering you to that particular company. Your insistence on this disclosure may change the agent's mind about giving you the referral. Note that it is against HUD rules for the seller to insist as a condition of sale that you use a particular title insurance company. (See Chapter 3.)

Is a method for prorating funds specified?

Owning a property involves ongoing costs. For example, taxes are owed 365 days a year. Hazard and fire insurance premiums are ongoing as are the mortgage payments if an existing mortgage is being assumed by the buyer. Consequently, the responsibility for these ongoing charges must be assigned properly and fairly when the property is sold. The method used to apportion those costs that are continuously paid is to prorate them. This simply means that the sellers will make payments right up to a certain date, after which you will take over. Your purchase agreement should specify the date of proration, which is typically the date that the escrow is closed. (This date is normally used because it's the date the title is transferred and, usually, the possession of the property as well.) The prorating can sometimes become confusing since the sellers may be entitled to money back. This occurs when the sellers have prepaid a cost, such as often happens with taxes or insurance. If you're not sure what items are to be prorated or as of what date, be sure to ask your agent to clarify this information.

QUESTIONS TO ASK YOUR AGENT AND/OR ATTORNEY

Is there any way I could lose my deposit?

Of course, there are normally many. You should find out exactly what the options are in your specific case. Be sure your agent and/or attorney rereads the purchase agreement so they understand exactly what's happening in your case and don't give you a generic answer. You should ask what will happen to your deposit in at least three separate situations: (1) What happens to the money if the deal goes through? Is it automatically counted as part of the purchase price? (2) What happens to the deposit if the seller backs out of the deal? Under what circumstances will I get my money back? Are there any circumstances in which the sellers might still get to keep it (for example, if you fail to close on time or can't come up with the promised down payment)? (3) What happens to the deposit if I decide to back out of the deal? Will I automatically lose it? Are there any circumstances in which I might get it back (for example, if the sellers can't give clear title or if there's a problem with the property)? Be sure to ask for the procedure for getting your deposit back (if it's in escrow, it may take both yours and the sellers' signatures to release it) and how long that will take.

Is there any way I could be sued?

Of course, at least in theory, anyone can sue anyone else at any time. However, you should ask your attorney what the chances are that the sellers might sue you in various circumstances. For example, what if you back out of the deal without the benefit of falling back on a contingency clause? (You can get financing, but you still refuse to go through with the purchase.) What is the likelihood of the sellers' suing you for "specific performance"—demanding that you complete the purchase? If they do sue and win, can they force you to complete the purchase, or are they more likely to get a monetary settlement? Are there any extenuating circumstances (such as the sellers' lying in their disclosures or failing to reveal problems with the home) that could mitigate in your favor? Be sure you understand all of the options and your liability in each case before you sign the purchase agreement.

Should I sign an arbitration clause?

An *arbitration clause* normally says that if there's a dispute between you and the sellers (or sometimes you and the agent), you agree in advance to binding arbitration as the process of settling it. Often agents and sometimes sellers will want you to sign this clause because it may tend to limit their exposure to large claims. However, sometimes attorneys will discourage you from signing it. They may say that it's generally not a good policy to sign away a right, in this case the right to sue the agent or sellers, in advance. It may turn out that, depending on what happens in the deal, you will want to sue the sellers if you were severely damaged (financially speaking). And arbitration normally does not allow for large damage or punitive damage awards. Be sure to take careful note of who you ask (your agent and your attorney) and listen carefully to the reasons they give for wanting you to sign, or not to sign, this clause. Keep in mind that it takes effect only if *both* you and the sellers sign.

Should I sign a liquidated-damages clause?

A *liquidated-damages clause* usually states that if you back out of the deal without cause (you can't exercise a contingency, for example, and simply want out—perhaps you found a better home to buy), your deposit is the full amount of the damages that the sellers can collect. In other words, the sellers can't sue you for specific performance, to force you to purchase the home or pay damages. Carefully quiz your attorney and/or agent on this clause. Sometimes it can be to your advantage to sign it. For example, if you put up a small deposit, you may be willing to lose it to simply get out of the deal. If you've signed this clause, presumably you can walk away with your pride intact, even if your wallet is somewhat lighter. Also carefully ask your attorney under what circumstances, if any, the clause might be declared void. In other words, what might you or the seller do in the transaction (such as fraud) to void the clause.

How should I take title?

There are many ways to take title, and each has different consequences both from a tax as well as a legal perspective. For example, you may take title with your spouse as *joint tenancy with right of survivorship.* This means that if one of you dies, the other automatically inherits the property. The wording *tenants in common* means that the other spouse or partner can bequeath their share to someone else. *Community property* has certain tax law advantages (such as a stepped-up basis upon the death of one spouse). Your state may also have additional methods of taking title. Be sure you talk with your attorney about your personal, financial, and tax situation so that he or she can recommend the best way for you to take title. Keep in mind that everyone's situation is different and many situations can involve complex tax and legal considerations. Do not simply read a book on the subject and make a hasty decision. Check out thoroughly with a professional the best way for you to take title.

Is there anything else I should watch out for?

This is a catch-all question that you definitely should ask. In reading through the purchase agreement, you, your agent, and/or your attorney may have caught something that needs to be dealt with that you (or I) didn't think of asking. Now's the time to get it out into the open. Not only should you ask about anything not yet discussed that you're unsure about but you should also ask if there's anything that your agent or attorney noted that's unusual or that requires additional information. Remember, the only dumb question is the one not asked.

Be sure to reread the boilerplate. Look to see if unwarranted charges to you, such as a transaction fee, have been added. Ask questions!

7

Home Inspection Tips & Traps

QUESTIONS TO ASK YOURSELF

Can I use the home inspection as a tool to get a lower price?

Many buyers do, although it's not strictly ethical. It's important to understand that in today's real estate transactions, a signed purchase contract is only one step along the way to a deal. Before that deal can be made, all of the contingencies to the contract must be removed. One common contingency is that you have the right to have the home professionally inspected and approve the inspection report. If the inspection uncovers problems that were not known or disclosed previously, you may be able to back out of the deal. Many buyers hire the toughest inspectors hoping to find many problems. They then use these problems as a wedge to force the sellers to make concessions in the price or terms of the deal.

Does the report show something unfavorable?

It's up to you to assess the seriousness to you of any problem reported by the inspector. If it's minor, you may simply want to ignore it. For example, leaking faucets are usually fixed by changing a washer. So this defect may not even be of sufficient concern to bring up to a seller. On the other hand, leaking pipes in the attic, walls, or—far worse—in the foundation or slab are a very serious problem. You most certainly want to discuss them with the seller. Remember that anything that's going to cost a lot of money to fix will affect the price of the property both when you buy it now and later on when you, in turn, decide to sell. If you don't get a major problem remedied by the seller now, you may have to pay to have it fixed either while you live in the property or before you resell.

Am I going to back out of the deal?

In a properly worded home inspection contingency, it is your right to back out of the deal if a serious problem is uncovered. It's up to you to decide whether you can live with the house *if* the problem is corrected or if the problem is so egregious that you simply no longer want the home. Before you decide to back out of the deal, however, you owe it to yourself to listen to any explanations the sellers may offer and to get several contractors to explain how the problem could be solved and how much it will cost. I've seen situations in which houses were slipping down the hillside, an obvious warning to back out of the deal. But contractors were consulted, and they said they could shore up the house to correct the current problems and prevent future ones, by which they were suggesting that the buyer go ahead with the deal as long as the costs could be negotiated.

Am I going to negotiate the cost of repairs?

You can present the sellers with the report indicating the problem. Then you can disapprove of the report, and with a properly drawn home inspection contingency, you can threaten to back out of the deal. Then, at virtually the same time, you can agree to go forward with the purchase, provided that the sellers will repair the problem to your satisfaction. Now you've batted the ball into the sellers' court. They must decide if they'll pony up the money to fix the problem. If it's a few hundred dollars, almost certainly they'll accede to your demands. On the other hand, if you want a new roof costing $25,000, they may balk. Now you can negotiate. Perhaps a new inexpensive roof will cost only $12,000. But the nice tile roof you want costs $25,000. If the sellers will pay up to $12,000, perhaps you're willing to pay the balance, or not, depending on how badly you want the house—and how good a negotiator you are.

Can I get a settlement in cash?

The problem with having sellers do any repair work is that the work will be done to their standards, not yours. And since they're leaving the property, chances are they'll get it done as cheaply as possible. Therefore, you may want to get a settlement in cash (usually in the form of a credit off the closing costs or even the down payment). Then, after the purchase is completed, you can do the work yourself—or not as you see fit. Keep in mind, however, that for this to be an effective ploy, you will need to accurately know how much the repairs will actually cost. Also, sometimes lenders will not fund a new mortgage until repair work is completed. For this reason, agents may sometimes want to handle repairs outside of escrow. This can be a risky business—check with your attorney.

Am I having a professional home inspection?

You should. Chapter 6 talks about your purchase agreement having a contingency clause regarding your right to withdraw from the deal if an inspection reveals previously undisclosed problems in the property. The professional inspection clause allows you to engage your own inspector to conduct on average a 2- to 3-hour examination of the property. While this amount of time is too short to cover everything, an amazingly large number of problems can be uncovered. Without this inspection, you'd be buying the home blind. With it, you have a much better idea of what you're getting. Think of it this way, if the inspector finds $50,000 worth of damage, would you still want to pay the full price you offered for the property? Or would you want to adjust your price down accordingly?

Am I selecting the inspector?

You should. You're paying for the inspection, and you should select the inspector, even if at the outset you don't know whom to select. If you allow the sellers to choose the inspector, how will you ever know whether or not they chose a friend who might have "overlooked" a few things? If you let your agent choose, how do you know he or she didn't choose an inspector not because he or she was particularly thorough but because he or she was known for giving homes good passing grades, thus making it easier to complete the sale? Only if you check out inspectors and pick one whom you believe to be the best qualified will you most likely have an inspection you can believe.

Have I examined the inspector's credentials?

You can accept your agent's recommendations of inspectors and choose one from among them. But also ask friends, associates, and relatives who recently purchased homes about the inspector they used and ask them if they would recommend that person. In general, you want someone who knows construction—not necessarily a contractor who may know only one area such as framing or plumbing but someone such as a retired city building inspector who knows it all. Second best would be someone with a degree in a related field such as a structural engineer. You can find a list of inspectors in the Yellow Pages of the phone book. Today there are many companies springing up that advertise their services. Call and talk to a representative. Ask about qualifications. Ask to see references, and then call several of the names you are given. It's very interesting to hear what someone has to say who had an inspection and then moved into the home—did unrevealed problems later crop up?

Is the inspector licensed?

While a few states now license inspectors, most don't. Ask your agent if your state licenses home inspectors, and if it does, be sure the person you choose is licensed. In states that do not license inspectors, keep in mind that anyone can hang out a shingle and call himself or herself an "inspector." I can, and even you can!

Does the inspector belong to a trade group?

There are two main national organizations and many state trade groups. The biggest trade group is the American Society of Home Inspectors (ASHI, *ashi.com*). It is working hard to bring up the standards of the home inspection field. There is also the National Association of Home Inspectors (NAHI, *nahi.org*). Check with your agent for the name of local trade organizations. While belonging to these organizations does not guarantee finding a competent home inspector, it at least does indicate that the person is attempting to be professional. Also see the Internet resources at the end of this book.

Have I agreed on a fee for the inspection?

As are most things in real estate, the inspection fee is negotiable. However, when the market is hot and there are a lot of home sales, the inspectors will be very busy and won't be very willing to talk about a reduced fee. On the other hand, when there are few sales, you may be able to negotiate the price downward. Just be careful that in the process of negotiation you don't anger the inspector to the point that he or she does a superficial job. Expect to pay between $200 and $350 depending on the area of the country and the size of the home. If you require additional inspections, say, from a soils engineer or a roofing or pool specialist, be prepared to pay extra for these. One thing that often shocks buyers is that these people usually want their money in cash, as soon as they've finished the inspection. Unlike most other services, they don't like putting a bill into escrow and waiting until the deal closes to get paid. (They're worried that if the deal doesn't close, they won't get paid!)

Should I go along during the inspection?

Perhaps the biggest mistake that buyers make is not going along with the home inspector. Of course, not wanting to go along is understandable: it takes time out of your busy schedule; the inspector often goes into the attic and under the house where things can be dirty and filled with critters (such as spiders and frogs—when it's wet); and in some cases crawling around can be physically challenging. However, there's one big overriding factor that speaks for going along—you can ask questions and get answers. While you will get a written report, often that report is filled with so many caveats and disclaimers that you can't tell whether the inspector is approving or disapproving of the property. However, inspectors are almost always far more open when you're along making casual conversation. They may be happy to tell you that the roof needs repair or replacement because of worn areas they'll show you while the written report may state, "Roof indicates some wear that may or may not require correction." Take the time, wear old clothes, and ask a lot of questions.

When will I see the inspection report?

That depends on how busy the inspector is. Today, most inspectors work out of an office that has secretaries to handle the reports. Typically the inspector will make notes while he or she is on the site, then go back to the office and dictate a report. A secretary will then enter the inspector's report as data into a computer program that will load the data into the right places and moments later spit out the report. If this is the way your inspector works, you could have the report back as quickly as the same day. On the other hand, if the inspector laboriously writes it out by hand, you might not have the report for a week. If your inspection contingency allows only 2 weeks, before you hire an inspector, you'll want to check first to be sure that he or she can get your report back to you quickly.

Can the inspector show the report to others?

In theory, you're paying for the report, so only you (and those you designate, such as your agent) can get it. However, many sellers will include an addendum to your inspection report contingency in the purchase agreement specifying that they are entitled to a copy of the report and may show it to anyone they choose. The sellers want the report in case you decide not to purchase the property. They may have a legal obligation to show any reports made on the property to future buyers, and you would put them into a real bind if you refused to release it to them.

Can I interpret all the caveats in the report?

The first things you're likely to notice in the written report are all the exclusions and disclaimers. The inspector will typically say that he or she is not responsible for any problems that were not visible—that is, any problems that were in inaccessible areas, such as in the walls, under the carpets, and behind furniture. Further, the inspector may disclaim responsibility for items not covered by the report. And the inspector may further disclaim liability for items that were covered but were misinterpreted for whatever reason. In one case, I saw a report in which the inspector disclaimed responsibility for negligence on his or her part! In other words, many inspectors play CYA with their reports. The reason is that over the past few years, buyers who had inspections later discovered problems with their homes that weren't uncovered by the inspector, and they have come back and sued their inspector. Further, when inspectors did point out serious defects with the property, sometimes sellers would sue them for knocking their house! To try to avoid this liability, the reports tend to be heavy on disclaimers. Further, they also often don't come right out and say anything definitively (see above).

Is the report thorough?

Simply reading it will give you a good idea. If the inspector generally says the electrical and plumbing systems are in good working order without actually mentioning anything that he or she checked, you would be suspicious. Or if the inspector reports finding a faucet that was leaking but doesn't indicate he or she checked the water heater or the rest of the plumbing system, you'd likewise be suspicious. You can also compare your report to the ASHI's Standards of Practice that suggests virtually everything an inspector should check on all the systems in your home. You can find the ASHI standards at *ashi.com.* The specific URL as of this writing was *ashi.com/customers/ standards.htm.*

Can I get more information?

Your initial home inspection may turn out to be only an introductory report. It may find one or more areas that need additional investigation. For example, it may note cracks in the roof supports. Now you'll want to get a structural engineer's feedback. Or it may indicate standing water in the basement. You'll probably want a soils report. To get these additional reports, ask your inspector for recommendations. Typically he or she will know of more specialized inspectors that can be called in. You can also ask your agent as well as check with local universities for experts in this area. Finally, there are always the Yellow Pages of the phone book. If the initial report finds problems, be sure to go back to the sellers and ask for more time. This usually is done by disapproving the report and signing a new inspection contingency for additional days or weeks. Most sellers are agreeable since they will have the problem no matter who is interested in buying the house.

Does my report cover a lead inspection?

Probably not, although the inspector may make comments about the possibility of lead in the paint if the house was built prior to 1978 (when lead-based paint was banned). However, the sellers must, by federal law, provide a prescribed signed statement about lead in the house along with a prescribed pamphlet detailing the hazards of lead in the home. However, the statement merely asks them to disclose whether or not they know if the home has lead paint. Most sellers really don't know, which is what they indicate, leaving you where you started. However, you normally have 10 days from the time you receive this report to back out of the transaction. During that time you can have a lead inspection of the property. There are specific companies that handle this. (Check with *hud.gov* for directions on finding one in your area.) Lead inspectors will take paint samples and have them analyzed. The results are typically yes for paint in homes built prior to 1978 and no for homes built after 1980. (There were a few years when builders were allowed to use existing quantities of lead-based paint.) The report, however, is expensive and can easily cost $300 or more.

Do I know my recourse if there's lead paint in the house?

If it's a big concern to you, you usually have three choices. You can back out of the deal, according to the lead contingency. If you're within the time frame allowed, normally you can do this without losing your deposit. Or you can demand that the seller have the lead paint removed. Removal, however, is a difficult process. The paint can't be burned off, as this releases lead smoke into the air. It can't easily be sanded off, as this releases lead dust into the air. And chipping likewise produces problems. Often the paint must be either chemically removed, or the lumber onto which it was painted must be removed to a toxic dump site! As you might imagine, the cost can be huge, and most sellers simply refuse to pay. Finally, you can negotiate a lower price with the seller and decide to live in the house with the lead paint hazard present, certainly not a good idea, particularly if you have small children.

Does the report cover asbestos inspection?

You can hope that it will. A good inspector will note any asbestos materials that he or she sees during the inspection. This may be significant since with asbestos, what you see is usually where there's a problem. (Asbestos that's sealed in or encapsulated is typically considered not to be a hazard.) If the inspector, or you, suspects asbestos, you can have a sample of the material in question analyzed. There are companies that handle this. Check *epa.gov/opptintr/asbestos* for more information. The report should come back quickly indicating if there's asbestos present. If there is, it should be either removed or encapsulated according to government guidelines. This will have to be done by an asbestos abatement company, and it will be quite expensive.

Does it cover black mold inspection?

A good inspector will report any black mold that he or she sees. (You'll also want to check your termite and/or pest report for indications of black mold.) Black mold is associated with moisture and is common in construction materials. I've talked to builders who indicate they've seen it on brand-new wood going back to the 1940s. In the past it was of little concern except as it rots wood, drywall, and the like and requires repairs. However, several high-profile lawsuits alleging allergies, diseases, and even deaths caused by black mold have brought it to the forefront of public interest. Today there's almost an hysterical concern about the fungus. Therefore, even if you're not worried about black mold, you should be concerned that a future buyer of your property might be. In other words, black mold can lower the property's value. Therefore, if it's found, it would be to your advantage to have it removed one way or another. *Note:* As of this writing, the Centers for Disease Control and Prevention (CDC) has not listed black mold as a serious health hazard. However, it is conducting tests, so black mold might be listed in the future.

Can I remove black mold myself after I buy the house?

I have, but that doesn't mean you will want to. If you're concerned, then hire one of the many pest removal companies that newly specialize in this field. Some will "bubble" your house or the infected area, come clothed in protective gear sometimes with special breathing apparatus, and endeavor to remove the mold. Usually they do a good job, although the removal may require extensive rebuilding of certain areas. You can be sure it will be very costly.

Does the report cover other hazardous material?

Environmental hazards in the home can be anything from radon to formaldehyde, from copper in the water system to BHT or other chemicals leaking out of the soil. While an alert home inspector may keep an eye out for this, it's unlikely that he or she would spot it (unless there was a clear visible symptom such as blue water indicating copper or a noxious odor indicating formaldehyde). However, your best resource here is usually your agent. Good agents tend to know the types of problems most likely to occur in their area. For example, if many homes nearby have radon gas problems, the agent should give you that information so that you can get a radon inspection. If your house does have radon (a radioactive gas seeping out of the ground associated with lung cancer and other lung diseases), a radon gas removal system can be installed typically for a few thousand dollars. Be sure to have the seller pay for this. If you're suspicious of any other environmental hazard, ask your agent. Also check with HUD (*hud.gov*) for information on what additional hazards might be present.

Does the inspection report cover water purity?

Don't expect it to. If you're connected to a public water system, it is assumed that the water is pure enough to drink. Such an assumption, however, may not be warranted. You may want to contact the water company and ask to see an analysis of the drinking water in your area. Almost certainly they can produce this information. From the report you can see what chemicals and toxins are present. As a result, you may want to install a water purification system for the home. But most sellers will not agree to pay for this since it's basically preventive in nature. If the property has a well, you will definitely want to get a water analysis report. (Your agent should be able to arrange this for you.) In private wells the most common problem is usually fecal material (often from a nearby septic tank) mixing with potable water. If the well does not produce pure water, you should call in an expert on wells to see if it can be cleared up, or if not, if a new clear well can be dug. Find out the cost, and negotiate payment with the seller. You may want to back out of a purchase if the sellers cannot provide pure drinking water.

Does the inspection report cover building department permits?

Again, don't expect it to, but consider it a plus if it does. A typical report will cover only the physical findings of the home inspector. It will not include an examination of the building permits at city hall. If it doesn't, you may ask your agent to do this for you, or you may want to do it yourself. The reason for checking is that if there's any new construction obvious on the property without a corresponding building permit on file, you can assume it was done without the benefit of permit. This can mean that the work done was substandard. Or, even if the work is not substandard, you can assume that at some time in the future another buyer, or even you if you do some renovation, may be required to bring the nonpermitted work up to current building code standards. This can be very expensive. You may want to ask the sellers to either rip out and replace all of the nonpermitted work or get a building permit and bring it up to code.

Is the report "clean," nothing unfavorable?

If there's nothing bad on the report, the tendency is to jump for joy and say that the house is safe to purchase. However, it's important to remember all those caveats and disclaimers written into the report. Typically, it covers only what the inspector was able to see in a couple of hours of looking at the house. When the report is "clean," it means only that nothing was found, not that there's nothing there. The house could still have serious undiscovered problems. However, a clean report does suggest that the house may be in good shape. If you're suspicious of something, however, you may want to call the inspector back, or even hire a new one. On a callback, if the inspector finds something that he or she originally overlooked, there is typically no fee to you. If, however, nothing untoward is discovered, you may be charged for a whole new inspection.

Do I need a time extension to approve the report?

Possibly. You may need to get additional specialty reports. Or, if it's a hot housing market, you may not be able to get a home inspector out to the site as fast as you thought. Or you may have thought the agent was going to handle this only to discover that the agent thought you were, and now time is running short. You can ask the sellers for an extension of the time to approve the report. With a reasonable explanation and reasonable sellers, these extensions are usually given. However, in a hot market, the sellers may decide to play hardball and refuse to give you an extension. In that case, you must either approve a report you may not yet have received or take a chance on losing the house—not a good situation to be in. The timing issue is why it's important to get that report completed ASAP.

QUESTIONS TO ASK MY AGENT

Can you recommend a good home inspector?

Real estate agents work day in and day out with professional home inspectors. Indeed, every house they sell needs a home inspection. So it is logical to ask them about finding a good home inspector. However, keep in mind that there's an inherent conflict of interest that the agent has to face. A really thorough inspector may find some defects in the property that could cause you to back out of the deal, costing the agent a commission. A more lax inspector might not find these problems, resulting in your going through with the deal, meaning the agent will get the commission. It would be so easy for an agent to recommend an inspector who is known to be lax (one who doesn't create problems) rather than one known to be exceedingly thorough. This is not to say that all agents will recommend "easy" inspectors—most are too ethical to do that. However, it won't hurt to thoroughly check out the recommended inspector, including calling up former clients on his or her recommendation list to see how well the inspector did.

Do you have any relationship with the inspector?

Real estate agents should have an arm's-length relationship with the home inspector. That means ideally that the inspector should not be financially involved with the agent; the agent's company should not have any ownership in the inspector's company, and vice versa. Furthermore, the inspector should not be a relative or close personal friend of the agent. The reason for this is obvious. If the agent has anything other than a strict arm's-length business relationship with the inspector, there's an incentive to cut favors. You might not end up with the objective inspection you anticipated. This is not to say that either the inspector or the agent would do anything to harm you, but why take chances? There are plenty of inspectors out there. And plenty of agents too.

Has this home had any previous inspection reports?

It's vitally important that you know about and have the opportunity to examine *all* previous inspection reports, no matter how old. The reason is that there could have been a serious problem with the property years ago that was corrected. However, the fix may not have been permanent, and the problem could potentially come back. This will influence your decision to buy and if you do, how much you're willing to pay. However, because the problem was corrected, a new inspection may not reveal it. Your agent should ask the sellers for copies of all previous inspection reports. (This demand should also be part of your home inspection contingency clause in the purchase agreement.) Most sellers do keep old reports and can provide them. Of course, sometimes such things do get lost. However, you may then want to have the sellers include in their disclosure a disclaimer that there was nothing adverse in old but now lost inspection reports.

Do you know of any property defects or other problems I should check out?

In many states (California, for example), the real estate agent is required to conduct a personal examination of the property and give a disclosure to the buyers stating any defects found. If the agent doesn't give this to you (or it's not required in your area), you should ask for it. This is not to say that the agent is more qualified to examine a property than a home inspector—he or she presumably isn't. But agents see properties every day and may recognize problems that you or the inspector might overlook. These could include obsolescence, nonpermitted improvements, external factors (such as seismic or flood problems), or anything else. A good agent will volunteer such information. But if or she does not, you should ask for it.

Can you help me interpret the written report?

Most agents will be happy to go over the written inspection report and try to explain anything you don't understand. After all, they have the benefit of having read dozens, perhaps hundreds, of such reports and can quickly pinpoint real problem areas, while alleviating your concerns about other areas that may be of little consequence. For example, if there's a problem with leaking galvanized steel pipes, they might point out that replumbing may be necessary at a cost of thousands of dollars. On the other hand, if the inspector finds a few plugs or switches that aren't working, he or she may be able to point out that replacement will take only a few bucks. You can utilize the agent's vast experience to help you interpret the inspection report. However, some agents are loath to do this because of liability issues. They're afraid that if they give you advice and you act on it, if the advice turns out to be wrong, you'll come back and sue them. Having a good, trusting relationship with an agent, as well as conveying to the agent that you believe he or she is doing his or her level best to help you, is your best assurance of getting the kind of information you need.

Will you help negotiate any repairs with the seller?

An agent's job doesn't end with the signing of the purchase agreement. Indeed, today that signing is often merely a first step along the way to actually getting the property transferred to your name. If the inspection report reveals serious problems that need repairs, the agent is the one to negotiate these for you with the seller. Be sure to keep your agent informed of the results of the inspection as well as any repair work that you deem necessary. Then ask your agent to negotiate for you with the sellers. The agent should go to the sellers, present the inspection report as well as your demands for repairs, and (we hope) get the sellers' acquiescence to do the work. Of course, sometimes sellers refuse, or they don't want to do the job at the level of quality you want it done. This is the time the agent earns his or her salt getting concessions from the sellers. And sometimes getting concessions from you!

Will you help renegotiate the price with the seller?

Sometimes it's not simply a matter of repairing this or that. It's that the home inspection report reveals defects that are large enough to affect the price of the home. For example, a report may reveal a utility easement along one side of the property where you had planned on putting up a new garage. Because of the easement, you can't build there. Now the property is worth less to you, although you still want to buy it. In a sense it's like going back to step 1. The deal needs to be renegotiated, and it's up to the agent to do this. You need to ask your agent to step up to the plate and get the sellers to lower their price in light of the inspection findings. A good agent will be able to get you a lower price, or perhaps have the sellers pay some of your closing costs, to compensate for the uncovered problem.

QUESTIONS TO ASK THE HOME INSPECTOR (WHEN YOU GO ALONG)

How much of the property will you cover?

Don't assume that your inspector is going to do a thorough inspection of all aspects of the property. Most inspectors right off the bat will say they won't look anywhere that's inaccessible, and that includes inside walls and under carpeting. However, you may ask the inspector to include areas that he or she might not otherwise have included in the inspection. For example, if you suspect a cracked slab, with the seller's permission, you may have the inspector pull back some wall-to-wall carpeting and padding to check it out. Or you may ask the inspector to crawl into a far recess of the attic if you suspect that the area was only partly insulated. Knowing what the inspector plans to cover can help you determine how thorough the inspection will be. And it can help you request additional areas be inspected.

Any big or small problems with the heating and/or air-conditioning systems?

The inspector will undoubtedly use a thermometer to check the difference in temperature between the air return (where air flows into the furnace and/or air-conditioner) and a vent (where air comes out). With the air-conditioner on, the difference should be several degrees, indicating that the air-conditioner is working. Be sure the inspector also checks the furnace's heat exchanger for holes or cracks that could leak noxious fumes into the house (and which can cost a thousand dollars or more to replace). Ask about the age of the units and how much life the inspector thinks they have left. This information can indicate how long it will be before you need to have them replaced, and you may want to factor these figures into the price you pay for the home.

Is there anything wrong with the roof?

If you get a solid "It's in good shape," you probably don't need to worry about it. However, if there is a problem, be sure you ask to see for yourself exactly what it is. The inspector may take you inside the attic and show you pin-pricks of light shining through holes in the roof. Or you may be shown asphalt shingles curving up, indicating heat damage. Or wood shingles blown off the roof. Or water stains on attic beams indicating leakage. It's important that you see exactly what the problem is so that you'll have a good idea of what's required to fix it when you get cost estimates. If there's a leaking valley that needs new flashing, you won't be taken advantage of by an unscrupulous roofer who tells you the entire roof needs to be replaced. (Most roofers are quite reputable; however, if you see the damage for yourself, you'll be able to judge what they say.)

Any serious cracks in the foundation?

Almost all foundations, indeed almost all cement structures, have cracks. Typically these are small hairline fissures that don't run deep. However, there are other more ominous cracks. Separations more than one-sixteenth of an inch may run through the thickness of the concrete. Offsets where the cement on one side of the crack is higher or lower than the other indicate significant ground shifting. V-shaped cracks that start out small at the bottom and expand as they go up suggest a split foundation. Ask your inspector to look for cracks, and when he or she finds them, to identify the kind of crack and tell you its significance. Some cracks can be ignored. Others mean that tens of thousands of dollars will need to be spent to shore up a foundation.

Are there rebars in the foundation?

Rebars are reinforcement steel bars that are put into foundations to increase the strength and stability of concrete. Without rebars, cement is much more likely to crack and if it does, break apart. With rebars, even if small cracks occur, the cement is likely to remain in place. Rebars should be inside all foundations. However, sometimes the builders leave them out either by accident or on purpose (to save money). You can detect rebars in concrete using a variety of metal detection equipment. However, if there's a significant crack in the concrete, the presence or absence of rebars can often be determined just by the trained eye. If your inspector indicates that he or she thinks the foundation lacks rebars, definitely get an engineering report perhaps including the drilling of inspection holes. Having a foundation without rebars is like having a building on shifting stones. Often to save the house, it will need to be raised and an entirely new foundation poured underneath, at a cost of many tens of thousands of dollars. *Note:* With new construction, fibrous concrete is sometimes used, which may reduce the number of reinforcing bars needed.

Any water damage?

Water damage can be indicated in many ways from simple stains to black mold to rotten timbers. A good inspector will carry a narrow flathead screwdriver along and will poke at wood near any source of water to determine whether it is solid or rotten. He or she will also check for mold and stains. If the inspector indicates there is water damage, it's most important to ask how serious it is. Often water damage can be cleaned away. Sometimes, however, it may require major repairs. Also ask what remedial steps should be taken to prevent future damage. The inspector may verbally suggest a drain or even a sump pump.

How are the fences?

An inspector giving you candid comments may say something like, "The fence posts have been in the ground too long, and they are rotting and need to be replaced. If it were me, I'd put in a whole new fence." (Fencing an average home can cost several thousands of dollars.) On the other hand, the written inspection report may state only that the inspector observed one or two fences posts leaning that may or may not suggest rotten wood. You can ask the inspector to check out several posts to see if they all are rotten or if only one or two are. Also ask about the condition of gates. If the yard has a pool or spa, undoubtedly the inspector will tell you that the gate needs to have an automatic shutting device on it to prevent its being accidentally left open. And the entire pool and/or spa area needs to be fenced up to local building code standards.

Any electrical problems?

The inspector should check all of the circuit breakers as well as individual switches and plugs. Be sure to ask about any specific problems. For example, a written report may say that because the house is old, it lacks *ground fault interrupter* (GFI) *plugs* in the kitchen and bath and that it doesn't have a ground wire running throughout the electrical system. However, when you're with the inspector, he or she may verbally tell you that the place is a death trap without that ground wire, and it needs to be installed, along with GFI plugs where appropriate, before anyone moves in. Further, you are looking at a complete revamping of the electrical system costing upward of $5000 or more. Go with the inspector; ask away.

Any plumbing problems?

Ask the inspector if the pipes are galvanized steel (with a life span of 25 to 50 years or so) or copper (with a longer life span). Ask the inspector how long it will be before any pipes need to be replaced, even if they appear in good condition now. Ask about the age of the water heater—and when it will need to be replaced. Ask if it's strapped down to prevent dangerous movement in storms or earthquakes. Ask about the water pressure. If it's too high or too low, ask about the cause and possible remedy. Also ask about the drains: How well do they work? Are any small stoppages apparent? How much will it cost to fix any problems found? Sometimes vegetation roots can block drain lines, a problem that may be very expensive to cure. A good inspector may be able to determine where the drain line goes from the house to the street and tell you the likelihood of tree roots being a problem. Feel free to ask any other questions that come to mind.

Any problems with any fixtures or appliances?

Any inspector worth his or her salt will turn on every appliance to see if it works or not. However, you can ask the inspector how old the appliances are, what their likely lifespan is, and how costly it will be to replace them. Also, sometimes though appliances work, they are in need of repairs. For example, a dishwasher may have rust spots on its walls, indicating that it may soon rust all the way through the leak. In that event, it would need to be repaired or replaced. An oven door may have a broken or torn seal, meaning that it won't heat well. Sometimes the seal can be replaced. Other times the door is tweaked and will need to be replaced. Ask the inspector about each appliance in the home and listen to the comments. Yes, they may work, but how well and for how long?

Any structural problems?

Some problems may be obvious, such as broken timbers or holes in the roof. Others may not be as easily seen. Ask the inspector to open and close all doors and windows. If they don't work well, does it indicate house shifting? And does that indicate damage? What about leaning? Ask the inspector to tell you if any of the walls are tilted rather than straight, which would indicate structural problems. Ask the inspector to sight along the surfaces of the home to look for any bulges, dips, or other irregularities indicating structural damage. A good inspector may be able to take a few keen looks at a home and tell you all kinds of stuff that he or she might not want to put into the written report because there's no solid evidence easily found to demonstrate it. However, the inspector's suspicions may be enough to warrant your calling in a structural engineer for a closer look.

Have you checked with the city for permits?

Many inspectors don't, but a few do. One inspector I knew would go down to the building department and have the city pull all the permits on a property before he showed up. Then when he arrived, he could tell which work was done with permit and which without. It was a real boon to the buyers. Be sure to ask if your inspector has done this. If not, don't expect him or her to do it. Most inspectors I've known won't do any additional inspection work after they've given the property its physical. Keep in mind, however, that there's nothing to prevent you from asking your agent to secure copies of permits (see above) or even to prevent you yourself from going down to city hall and getting them. They are, after all, public information.

Should I have a survey?

A land survey will show you where the property lines are. It should also reveal many easements and other items that could affect the property. Your inspector should be able to tell whether your property is a good candidate for an inspection. If you're in an urban area where the lots are very well delineated, he or she may suggest not spending the money for the survey (which can easily cost $300). On the other hand, if you're in a rural area, or if the house seems overly close to an apparent lot line, or if there is anything else to suggest that all is not as it should be, the inspector may indicate you should go ahead with the survey. Some inspectors believe that surveys should be done on all properties with no exceptions, just to be sure. If the survey turns up a problem, you will want to be sure to have it corrected by the sellers before you take title. These problems can be nasty and can require attorneys and title clearance reports to get rid of. Better to let the seller do it than you.

Any other problems I should know about?

This is, obviously, a catch-all question to cover anything that the inspector didn't mention. You should ask it after the inspection has been completed. However, don't assume that the inspector will say, "No, I think we've covered it all." Just as likely, the inspector may say something such as, "Well, now that you ask, there's something that's been bothering me but which I didn't want to bring up . . . " and then go on to point out some feature, such as the lay of the land that allows water to settle in the property, or the condition of the stucco, or any of a hundred other things. Always ask this question, and give your inspector a last chance to provide you with more important information.

3

Obtaining the Financing to Close the Deal

8

Finding a Good Lender

QUESTIONS TO ASK YOURSELF

Why do I need a lender to close?

Unless you're paying cash for your property, you will need a mortgage to close your deal. This mortgage will be the difference between what you're putting down in cash and the balance of the price. If you're buying a home for $100,000 and putting $10,000 down, you'll need a mortgage for $90,000. Of course, you'll also need to have the cash to pay for closing costs (or finance those costs).

Have I specified the mortgage I need?

Your purchase agreement should detail the mortgage including:

- Full amount of mortgage
- Maximum interest rate you'll pay
- Term (10 years, 15 years, 30 years, or other terms)
- Type (fixed interest rate, variable rate, hybrid)
- Maximum points you'll pay

It's important that this all be spelled out and that it be written in the form of a contingency. Thus, your purchase agreement would state that your purchase of the property was "subject to" your getting the specified mortgage. This way if for some reason you could not get the mortgage, you would not be obligated to continue with the purchase and should, presumably, be able to get your deposit back.

Have I found a lender?

Because getting financing is such an integral part of purchasing a home today, you should find a lender long *before* you even begin to look at property. Lining up a lender will allow you to be preapproved (see below), which has two big advantages. First, by submitting a credit report, detailing your assets including cash on hand, and describing your income, the lender can tell you how big a property you can afford. Thus, you'll know your price range. Second, the lender can give you a letter of preapproval that will help convince a wary seller that you can, indeed, afford the property your are bidding on. Today, almost every buyer comes in with some sort of preapproval letter.

Am I preapproved?

This means that a lender has examined your qualifications to get a loan and based on that, has determined the amount of a mortgage you can qualify for (usually given as a maximum monthly payment). Today, a good preapproval letter will specify the following:

- The monthly payment you can afford to make on a mortgage. This is important because as interest rates go down, your monthly payment will allow you to obtain a bigger mortgage. Unfortunately, as rates rise, the mortgage you can afford will decrease.
- The level of your preapproval:
    - *Highest.* The lender has verified your income, assets, and credit and is ready to fund.
    - *Middle.* The lender has verified your credit and, assuming your assets and income are as you state, will fund.
    - *Lowest.* The lender's representative (usually a mortgage broker—see below) has taken a verbal application from you and based on that,

has issued the letter. No funding will occur
unless and until the lender approves your
credit, assets, and income.

- The term of the letter—usually a month or two.

You can use this preapproval letter to convince a seller
to agree to your purchase offer. Of course, the higher the
level of preapproval, the better chance you have. After you
succeed in getting a seller to sign a purchase agreement,
you can go back to the lender and seek funding of the loan,
something that can take anywhere from a few days up to
45 days, depending on what problems occur. You are not
usually obligated to go back to the lender who gave you a
preapproval. However, if you unwisely paid a fee for this
normally free service or contractually agreed to go with the
original lender, you may feel obliged to.

Have I checked out different lenders?

All money is the same. Lenders, however, are different.
Some are simply businesspeople out to make a buck and
in so doing, provide a valuable service to you. A few can
be predatory. You need to beware of the latter. While they
often advertise lower-than-market interest rates, after
you add in points and garbage fees (see Chapters 1 and
2), their true costs can be significantly higher. A recommendation from a friend, associate, relative, or other person *not affiliated with the particular lending company* is often
a good reference. A real estate agent may also be able to
recommend a good lender. Be wary, however, of agents
who may recommend a lender with whom they have a
financial arrangement. (See "controlled business arrangements" in Chapter 3.) Also, demand to see *all* costs up
front before even applying for a mortgage.

Have I checked out a mortgage broker?

A mortgage broker is to a loan what a real estate broker is
to property. Indeed, most mortgage brokers also hold real
estate agent licenses, although they may hold an additional license for lending. Mortgage brokers "contract"
with a wide variety of lenders. They become the retail
outlet for those lenders. For example, a bank in Vermont

may want to make a mortgage in California. It has no offices in California, so it makes arrangements with a mortgage broker to secure loans for it. For this the Vermont bank pays the mortgage broker a fee, typically 1 to 1.5 percent of the loan amount. Of course, it could be a bank in the same state as the mortgage broker, or even a consortium of investors (such as insurance companies) who have pooled their money and intend to make real estate loans. The mortgage broker then goes out and secures mortgages from people like you. He or she takes the application and forwards it to the lender who arranges for underwriting, if necessary. The mortgage broker also arranges for an appraisal of the house, gets the credit report, and secures all of the paperwork necessary to obtain the loan, and ultimately sees that the documents you need to sign are delivered to the escrow holder. This is how he or she earns the fee.

Have I avoided paying a broker's fee?

As noted above, the lender pays the mortgage broker's fee directly. That does not mean, however, that some mortgage brokers will not attempt to charge you an additional fee. Usually there is nothing illegal about this. Unfortunately, as of this writing, they usually do not have to disclose the fee they are earning directly from the lender (this should change in the near future), and some unscrupulous brokers have demanded an additional fee from borrowers sometimes claiming that this is their only source of income. If you pay the mortgage broker, chances are he or she is getting paid twice. When looking for a mortgage broker, the first thing you should ask is if he or she is charging you a fee. The only acceptable fees up front for the buyer to pay are for an appraisal (between $200 and $350) and a credit report (usually under $50). Most good mortgage brokers will absorb the credit report fee if you go ahead and get the financing through them.

Have I checked out a mortgage banker?

Note that mortgage *brokers* (above) do not lend you their own money. Rather, they act as brokers for the actual lenders. On the other hand, some lenders make direct loans. Think of a mortgage *banker* as a bank that has no checking or savings accounts, no commercial accounts, and usually no retail offices. Its sole business is to make mortgage loans, which it funds from its own capital. (It then usually packages the loans in groups and resells them on the secondary market to Fannie Mae or Freddie Mac.) Most mortgage bankers are simply another lender for mortgage brokers to use. When you apply for a mortgage from your mortgage broker, he or she may be getting it from a mortgage banker. However, in some areas of the country, mortgage bankers go directly to the public. Thus, you might avoid a mortgage broker and get a loan directly from a mortgage banker. Keep in mind that this will not usually save you money. The mortgage banker will not normally share with you the fee it would otherwise pay a mortgage broker. There is no harm, and probably no advantage, in dealing directly with a mortgage banker.

Have I searched for a good mortgage lender?

As noted above, try to get a recommendation from a person you know is *not* affiliated with the lender you are considering. You can also try the Yellow Pages in the phone book. Look under *banks* and *mortgage brokers.* And try the Internet. Many mortgage brokerage companies operate exclusively through their Web sites such as *eloan.com* or *mortgage.com,* which means that you can even get a loan online.

Have I tried getting an online mortgage?

It can be faster, but sometimes it is more difficult. If all of the materials you need to qualify are readily available, then the online lender can handle qualifying your loan in a matter of hours. The usual materials you need to qualify are an online credit report, online appraisal (yes, for some homes these are available!), bank check for deposits you have on hand, and online check with your employer. On the other hand, if these are not available via the Web, you will need to obtain them and spend a lot of time mailing things in. Also, some escrow companies will not work with online lenders, and this could lead to complications with the seller and/or the agents involved in the deal.

Have I tried a bank or credit union?

By all means, do! Sometimes banks run special real estate financing deals. Try the big ones first (Bank of America, Wells Fargo, Citibank, etc.), and then also try some local banks in your area, the latter if you've got some special problem that they are more likely to understand because they live in your community. Credit unions may also make some real estate loans, usually second mortgages. Their big advantage is that the interest rate they charge could be more competitive. However, sometimes the hoops you must jump through and the garbage fees they attach offset this.

Have I avoided paying an advance fee?

Your goal is to get money from the lender, not to give money to it. Except for credit reports and appraisal fees, most lenders will not charge you anything to secure financing through them. Beware of a mortgage broker or other lender who wants money up front to secure a mortgage for you. Once you pay the money (it could be $1000 or more), you are locked into this lender. If you go elsewhere, you may lose the money you paid. If this lender then wants to charge you a higher-than-market interest rate or lots of garbage fees, you are caught. Either you pay, or you lose your advance fee. Sometimes unscrupulous lenders charge advance fees when interest rates are dropping and there is a surge of borrowers who are afraid they won't be able to find a lender. Don't worry because, since time immemorial, there have always been plenty of lenders.

Should I check out my own credit?

Yes, this is usually a good idea. You can apply for a credit report on yourself from any one of the three national credit reporting bureaus for a nominal fee (see the Internet Resources at the end of this book). When you get your credit report, check to be sure all the facts, such as your name, address, social security number, and employment information, are accurate. Also check to be sure that all of the reports from lenders are accurate. For example, an old lender may have overlooked sending a report that you successfully paid off a loan. Or a lender may have said you are late in payments when you aren't. You should challenge this in the credit report (the bureau will tell you how), and more important, you should go back to the original lender and demand they clear up the problem, which almost all will do. Clearing up blemishes on your credit report can mean the difference between qualifying for the loan you need to buy the property you want or being turned down.

Have I checked out my FICO score?

FICO is the acronym for Fair Isaac. This company evaluates credit reports, and it is used by the majority of lenders. When you think about it, a credit report only states facts. It doesn't draw conclusions. FICO looks at a credit report and then using computer models based on thousands of successful and unsuccessful borrowers, gives an opinion. That opinion is in the form of a score between 350 and 900. The lenders send your credit report to FICO and then read the score that is returned. The higher your score, the more likely you are to get good financing. Also, the higher your score, the lower your interest rate is likely to be. You can obtain your FICO score along with an explanation of how it was derived by going to *www.myfico.com*. Today FICO scores in the mid 600s and higher will usually qualify you for a *conforming loan*, one that conforms to the underwriting standards of Fannie Mae or Freddie Mac and one that offers the best terms and interest rate.

Has my loan been approved?

Once you've been preapproved, have made a deal to purchase a property, and have applied to the lender for the loan, there will be a period of time while the lender checks out you and the property. Typically lenders will come up with some objections to you. In my experience, unless you actually have a real credit problem, these objections are often inane. They may want you to prove that you actually paid off an old loan, even though you have already given them documentary evidence of that fact. They may claim you have another name, which you've never heard of. They may want you to prove that you haven't worked for someone else for the last 2 years. The trouble with these demands is that proving a negative can be very difficult. In the end, often the lender will simply stop asking stupid questions and move forward. It will approve your mortgage. When that happens, it's ready to fund. And you're ready to close the deal.

How close to the actual closing can I switch lenders?

Sometimes lenders won't fund for unclear reasons (see above). Sometimes lenders won't fund because of credit problems you have. Sometimes lenders add on unexpected garbage fees that you don't want to pay. For all of these reasons, it may come down to the last few days before closing when you suddenly realize you can't live with the lender you've got. You realize that the only way to avoid exorbitant fees or to actually get the money is to switch to a new lender. The big problem here is time. The sellers are ready to close. You've probably signed a purchase agreement with a time clause in it, and time has just about run out. You only have two real courses of action. Try to get the existing lender to fund and/or pay the excessive fees and close the deal. (This is why you should have negotiated these fees when you first applied.) Or you can try to quickly bring in a new lender. The problem here is that any new lender will take time to approve you. However, in today's electronic age with no problems showing up, a mortgage might be arranged in as little as a few days. Check with a good mortgage broker or an online broker.

Will the seller object if I try to switch lenders?

The seller doesn't really care where you get the money from, just that you close the deal. If you can't close on time (as agreed upon in your purchase agreement), the seller could quash the deal—and demand to keep your deposit, and even sue you! Of course, if the reason is that your lender won't or can't fund, then the loan contingency clause your agent wrote into your purchase agreement (your agent did do this, didn't he or she?) should protect you (see Chapter 5). On the other hand, if the lender is ready to close but you're balking over garbage fees, you could be in trouble with the seller. Your loan contingency might not protect you here. However, always keep in mind that the seller's prime motivation is usually to sell the property. Unless there's another better qualified buyer waiting in the wings with a backup offer, chances are the seller will give you the few days you need to work things out. The seller usually wants the sale too. Some agents recommend simply not telling the seller the problem and quickly trying to get other financing. My own feeling is that withholding this information breeds mistrust, which can be deadly to the deal if it takes you more than just a few days to get a new lender. My suggestion is that, in most cases, you simply explain what's happening and throw yourself on the mercy of the seller. Most people understand, and they, too, are angered by garbage fees or lenders who can't or won't fund. Almost always you can buy yourself a few more days this way. When it drags on for weeks, however, even the most understanding seller will eventually pull the plug. Which is to say, if at all possible, get a good lender at the beginning.

9
Finding Just the Right Loan

QUESTIONS TO ASK YOURSELF

Do I understand the differences between the mortgages available to me?

☐

Most people are concerned with only two things: the amount of the loan and the monthly payment. Yet, the terms can be vitally important. They may provide that the monthly payment goes up over time (a variable-rate loan). Or they could demand a payoff penalty when you refinance. Or the amount of the mortgage could actually increase so that you owe more at the end of the loan term than when you started. When you shop for a mortgage to close the deal, it's important to consider all aspects of the loan.

Is my application appropriate for my state?

☐

Applications vary dramatically from state to state. Any lender in your state should provide you with what your state requires. Sometimes you will have to read information on loans and then sign a form that says you've been given that explanation before a lender can even take your application or quote a rate. In other cases, there are no restrictions, and the lender can move forward quickly. Federal regulations provide that you must be given a Real Estate Settlement Procedures Act (RESPA) good-faith estimate form at the time you apply for a loan.

Am I getting a *reduced-interest-rate, owner-occupied mortgage?* ☐

The lowest interest rate and best terms in home mortgages are offered to buyers who intend to occupy the home they purchase. Therefore, if at all possible, plan to move into your home. While this is a matter of "intent," the lenders and the government that oversees them want to be sure that you do move in. Some lenders will actually come knocking at the door after a month or so to see that you are there. Others will send loan packets with "no forwarding" only to the home address. Of course, the question becomes how long you have to occupy the property in order to qualify for the mortgage. There are no set rules here; however, most real estate agents will tell you at least a year, possibly two. Of course, if there are extenuating circumstances such as a job change, that time could be significantly shorter.

Am I getting a *first-time-buyer loan?* ☐

If you qualify as a first-time buyer, you may be able to get a mortgage with a smaller down payment and more liberal terms as well, and sometimes, at a reduced interest rate. Your mortgage broker can introduce you to these loans. (Or check with my book *How to Buy a Home When You Can't Afford It.*) Are you a first-time buyer? Usually you are if you haven't bought or owned a home in the past 3 years. If you owned property prior to that time, it probably does not disqualify you from claiming first-time-buyer status.

Have I tried getting an *assumable loan?* ☐

In this case, you assume a mortgage that already exists on the property, hopefully at the old, lower interest rate. The problem is that most modern loans, with the exception of some VA and FHA loans, are not assumable. Or if they are, you have to qualify for them as if you were applying for a new loan, and once you get them, the interest rate is bumped up to the current market levels. If you find an old FHA or VA loan that is assumable, given the recent appreciation in the housing market, it may be for only a small fraction of the home's value. (It could have been for nearly all the value when it was put on the property, but the value of the home has risen while the loan has gone down.) If the loan is valuable to you, for example, it might have a low interest rate and no qualifying, you may want to assume it and then give the seller a second mortgage for the balance. (Or get a new second mortgage from a lender.)

Have I tried getting an *equity loan?*

Many home buyers will actually get two new loans when they purchase a property. The first will be a large first mortgage to cover most of the costs of the purchase. The second will be a smaller home equity loan in the form of a second mortgage, often with a revolving line of credit. This allows them to withdraw some of their equity in the future. Usually, this works only when the large first mortgage is less than 80 percent of the value of the property. For example, you put 30 percent down, and you get a 70 percent new first mortgage, and a 10 percent equity line of credit. Note that most lenders will not offer you an equity loan unless your equity is over 20 percent. However, with rapid price appreciation that often happens fairly quickly, even if you can't get the equity loan when you buy, you may be able to get it only a few months (or years) later.

QUESTIONS TO ASK YOUR LENDER

Will you give me a *lock-in?*

A loan with a *lock-in* fixes the interest rate that you will be charged for the mortgage. It often takes 30 days or more to close escrow, and in that time the interest rates could change. Obviously, if rates go down, you'll be thrilled. But if they go up, it means you'll have a higher monthly payment that you might not be able to qualify for, and that could mean you'd lose the deal. Getting a lock-in supposedly guarantees that the rate at the end will be the same as at the beginning. The term of the lock-in varies lender by lender and also by the condition of the market. When rates are rapidly rising, a 15-day lock-in may be all that you can get. When rates are relatively stable, a 30-day or even 45-day lock-in may be possible. Sometimes lenders will demand a payment to put the lock-in in place. For example, for putting a lock-in on the loan, they may want one-eighth of 1 percent. On a $100,000 mortgage, that's $250. Whether or not you pay for your lock-in, be sure to get it in writing with the lender's authorized signature on the document. Otherwise, if interest rates really jump up, it's too easy for the lender to forget that you were locked in. Also ask what happens if the lock expires and if a lock fee is refundable.

Can I assume the existing loan?

You can ask the seller, but often the seller does not know or may have erroneous information. If you are seriously involved in purchasing a property, and an assumption is the way you want to go, contact the existing lender directly and determine if it will allow an assumption and if so, under what conditions and for what fee. Sometimes lenders won't talk to outside parties, so you may need to have the sellers do this for you.

Are you getting a rebate?

Depending on the interest rate you are charged, lenders either charge a premium to get the mortgage (points and other fees) or rebate money back. For example, if the current interest rate is 6 percent and you are applying for a 6.25 percent mortgage, there may be a rebate, say a thousand dollars, to the borrower. This money can go toward paying your other closing costs. One of the reasons for accepting a slightly higher-than-market rate for the loan is to get the rebate. Check with your mortgage broker.

Can I get a *no-qualifying loan?*

While much has been said about the need to qualify for a mortgage, sometimes it is not necessary. Some lenders offer loans where you do not have to submit a credit report and do not have to verify your income. You do, however, have to submit an application on which you state your income. Typically this is the case when loans are for less than 80 percent of the value of the property. Here, the lender is loaning more on the property's value than on your financial strength. Also, expect to pay a sometimes significantly higher interest rate for the additional risk. Finally, if in the future you should default on the loan, the lender may go back to the original application where you stated your income, and if it was greatly exaggerated, go after you for fraud. These types of loans come and go depending on market conditions. (They tend to appear when lenders are more desperate to get their money out.) Any good mortgage broker can tell you about them.

Can I get a *low-doc loan?*

These loans are usually available and are preferred by people who are self-employed and have trouble showing their true income. Traditionally the self-employed must show at least 2 years of 1040 tax returns to prove their income and must demonstrate that they have successfully been in the same line of work for many more years. The problem that some self-employed individuals have is that they may have been in business for less than 2 years. Or a substantial portion of their income was cash and not reported. This is a problem between the borrower and the IRS, and it needn't necessarily be a problem when getting financing. The low-doc loan requires only a credit report and verification of money on hand to make the down payment. It does not require verification of income. Again, however, if later on you allow the loan to go into foreclosure, the lender can come back and go after you for any fraudulent statements you made on the applications.

What is a *late-payment charge?*

All modern mortgages have a late payment charge. It varies, however, from mortgage to mortgage. Since there's always a chance that at some time in the future one or more of your payments could be late (you might forget, the mail could be delayed, you could have financial problems), you'd like this charge to be as small as possible. Typically it's around $50. However, in many mortgages it's 5 or 10 percent of the monthly payment. While you probably won't want to switch lenders just on the basis of a high late-payment charge, if it's very high, you may question it. Is the lender planning on "losing" some of your payments in the mail and making some extra money on late payment charges? Some borrowers feel this has happened to them in the past.

What is a *finance charge?*

To determine your finance charge, you want to know how much interest you are paying, including points. This is probably *not* the interest rate that you were quoted when you first asked about the loan. It is the annual percentage rate (APR) that is specified in your loan documents. The initial interest rate is typically quoted as something like, "6 percent interest plus 3 points." However, when you factor in the points plus other interest charges involved in the deal, the true interest rate may be 6.5 percent. This is what the APR will quote.

What is an *APR?*

As noted above, this is the interest rate you will be paying based on a very strict formula created by the federal government. It takes into account the stated interest rate on the loan, but it also factors in some points and fees that you may be charged. It's probably the closest you can come to the actual interest rate of your mortgage.

What interest rate is the amount of my monthly payment based on?

Your monthly payments are *not* usually based on the APR. Rather, they are usually based on the initial interest rate you were quoted. For example, if you're quoted "6 percent plus 3 points," your monthly payments are based on 6 percent interest, not the APR of the mortgage (which takes into account the points). Remember, the points and fees are paid one time when you close the deal. You can think of them as prepaid interest, although technically they may not be considered that. They are not calculated into the monthly payment that you make.

What is the *amount financed?*

This is the total amount of your mortgage. If you're borrowing $100,000 to buy a home, this is the amount financed on which you'll owe interest and make monthly payments. If your lender allows you to include some of the closing costs in the financing, it could be more. For example, if your closing costs are $5000, the amount financed could be $105,000 in our example. This, however, may not be the amount of money the lender actually advances. If you are charged 3 points on a $100,000 mortgage, the lender will advance only $97,000 (yet, you still pay as if you had received the full $100,000). You must come up with the $3000 in our example out of your pocket as closing costs. (Also reread Chapter 2.)

What is the *total of payments?*

If you have a 30-year loan, you will have 360 payments. The lender adds all these together to give you a total of all your payments. On a $100,000 mortgage it may come to something like $230,000. If you now subtract the mortgage amount ($100,000), you can determine the total interest ($130,000) you'll pay over 30 years. You can make this calculation yourself, although it won't be 100 percent accurate because usually the last payment is off a bit. To find the total of payments, simply multiply your monthly payment by the number of payments. On a 15-year loan, your total will be 180 payments; on a 10-year loan, 120 payments and so on.

What is a *fully amortized loan?*

This simply means that the mortgage is paid off in equal installments with no one payment higher than the others—no "balloon" payment. Most first mortgages are constructed this way. However, lenders of late have been offering "interest-only" first mortgages. (These have long been offered as second mortgages.) Here, you pay only the interest as it occurs monthly. However, at the end of the term, you still owe the full amount you originally borrowed. Some home buyers are persuaded to take this type of mortgage because it reduces their monthly payments slightly. Be aware, however, that it can be a trap. If you are forced to sell early and prices haven't appreciated, you could end up being *upside down* owing more to sell your property (when commission and closing costs are added in) than it's worth.

What is a *variable-rate loan?*

Here the interest rate varies depending on market conditions. It is usually tied to an independent index, such as the Treasury bill rate or the cost of funds to banks or even London Interbranch Borrowing Rate (LIBOR) used by British banks to determine their cost of funds. In most of these mortgages, as the rate goes up, so too does your monthly payment, although the loan may be written in such a way that these adjustments are made infrequently (every 6 months or more) and can go up only by limited steps (for example, 1 or 2 percent per adjustment). As interest rates go down, so too does your monthly payment. There are hundreds of varieties of variable-interest-rate loans. Be sure you ask your lender to thoroughly explain how yours works. Also, have an agent or other experienced person explain the "fine print" for any adverse terms the lender may have glossed over.

What is a *payment cap?*

In some variable-rate loans, the monthly payment is *capped*, meaning that it can only go up in a very limited way regardless of how high the interest rate soars. However, the interest rate lost to the lender with a payment cap is typically added to the principal of your loan (called *negative amortization*). Thus, even though your monthly payment remains relatively constant, the loan amount grows.

Will my loan be in the form of a *deed of trust?*

Trust deeds are the form of mortgage instrument preferred by lenders in most of the United States today. The reason is that they provide for quick foreclosure in the event that you don't make your payments. With trust deeds, lenders do not need to go to court to foreclose. Further, trust deeds give you relatively little time to redeem your loan in the event of a foreclosure. In California, for example, after a notice of default is filed, which gives *constructive notice* (it's recorded) that you're behind in your payments, you have 90 days to pay up all back payments and penalties to make the loan good. If you fail to do this, then there's a 2-week period of redemption in which you can save your property by paying off the loan in full. Finally, your property is sold to the highest bidder "on the courthouse steps," and you have no rights to redeem it. Other states have different time periods, but all are relatively short. With a trust deed there are three parties. You (called the *trustor*), the beneficiary (who is the lender), and a trustee who holds the deed and signs it over to the beneficiary in the event of foreclosure. Note that in this procedure, there is no need to go to court, although under most trust deed loans, the lender can opt to do this if it thinks it can collect a *deficiency judgment* from you. This means that the lender can go after you personally if your property doesn't bring enough to satisfy the loan amount at foreclosure.

Will my loan be in the form of a *mortgage?*

This is the other, older instrument used to make loans on real estate. It is still used in some states. There are two parties to it: you (the mortgagor) and the lender (the mortgagee). If you default and don't make your payments, the lender must go to court to secure a foreclosure. While these types of court proceedings are usually put at the head of the list, it still usually takes more time to foreclose than a trust deed. Additionally, you can always show up and give your story of woe to the judge, who may extend you more time. Finally, even after your property is sold on the courthouse steps, you may have a period of time in which to redeem it, sometimes as long as a year. From the borrower's perspective, a mortgage is probably a safer instrument. However, it is very hard to get a lender to use one.

Will my loan be sold?

Probably. Although you may get a mortgage from XYZ lender, there's really nothing you can do to keep it from being "sold" to ABC lender. Indeed, if you keep the mortgage over a period of years, you may find that it's "sold" many times. The term *selling* is somewhat misleading. The mortgage may actually have been sold in the secondary market to Fannie Mae or Freddie Mac. However, the servicing of the loan, which means getting the payments from you, charging late penalties, and handling foreclosure, is what the different mortgage lenders with whom you deal with do. Thus you may originally be serviced by XYZ lender only to have your loan turned over to ABC lender and later on to LMN lender—and on it goes. In each case the mortgage lender servicing your loan has all the rights and power of the original lender. However, because of the confusion such transfers sometimes cause with borrowers, today lenders are usually required to notify you in advance of the "sale" of your mortgage, and both the new and the old company are required to handle your payments for an overlapping period of time so that you don't inadvertently send your money to the wrong company and get a late-payment notice.

Will I have to sign a *Form 4506* (a tax form)?

Probably. And chances are this form will not be filled out when you sign it, although it should be dated. This form allows the lender to go directly to the IRS to confirm your income by means of past 1040 statements. The idea is to check to see whether or not you were entirely forthcoming on your loan application. Some lenders do this on a spot-check basis; others do it whenever there's a problem within the first few months—for example, if you did not make your payments. This form is good for 60 to 90 days from the date you sign it. I know I always hesitate to sign such a form because I don't want to give anyone the right to go poking about in my relations with the IRS. However, refusal to sign the form usually means the lender will not fund the loan, so you're over a barrel here. *Note:* If the form is not dated, I always date it and indicate that the lender can only secure 2 years worth of tax returns. Your lender may or may not allow this.

Will I get a *truth-in-lending disclosure*?

The lender must provide this disclosure to you usually within a few days of taking your loan application and certainly by the closing date. It will give you such vital information as the total number of payments, the total amount you'll pay, the mortgage amount, the total interest, and the annual percentage rate (APR). Lenders should be "right on" with the amounts they give you in this statement.

Will I get a *good-faith estimate?*

Yes, the Real Estate Settlement Procedures Act (RESPA) requires that a good-faith estimate be given to you within a few days after you have filed a mortgage application. However, be aware that no matter what the lender says on it, the fees can change by closing. And as of this writing, there is very little enforcement by the federal government of even gross changes between the estimate and the final closing costs.

Will I get a *servicing disclosure?*

This information simply tells you who will be servicing your mortgage. You can assume that the lender from whom you are borrowing your money is the servicer, to whom you'll make your mortgage payments. But sometimes lenders "sell" the mortgage to another servicer right after the closing. Therefore, your closing instructions may indicate that a different lender will be receiving your monthly payments. Be sure that you have the correct address and the correct loan number to send with your payment to whomever you are making payments. Otherwise, your payment may go astray and you could be hit with a late penalty.

What is the *HUD booklet?*

The Department of Housing and Urban Development (HUD) has prepared a home buyer's booklet. It contains information about negotiating a purchase, finding an agent, and handling the closing, and it also gives some of the fees you are likely to incur. It's a small booklet and can easily be read in a few minutes. Any lender providing a mortgage that involves the government in any way is required to give this booklet to you. If the lender doesn't, you can obtain the booklet directly from HUD (see the address in the Internet Resources section at the end of this book).

4

Closing the Escrow

10

Finding a Reliable Escrow–Title Insurance Company

QUESTIONS TO ASK YOURSELF

Why do I need to find an escrow–title insurance company?

You need to get title insurance to protect yourself from title problems on the property (and because your lender demands it). You need an escrow company to have an independent stake holder to process the closing, to accept monies and make distributions, and to record documents including the deed. In most states escrow companies and title insurance companies are one in the same, or they are at least affiliated so that it's one stop for you. (See Chapter 3 for an explanation of what title insurance is.)

What can go wrong with an escrow–title insurance company?

The tendency is to think that all such companies are alike. Nothing could be further from the truth. While the services they all perform are similar, some do it well and others do it badly. Here's a list of complaints sometimes heard about escrow–title insurance companies:

- *The escrow officer is difficult to reach and rude when I try to talk to her or him.* The reason for the officer's rudeness may not be that you're a pest, as the title officer may suggest, but that he or she is handling too many closings to give quality time to any one of them. Good escrow officers, with assistants, might handle 10 a day. They simply don't have time to continually explain the same thing to each new buyer. Faced with a tight schedule, they become quick, don't answer calls, and are sometimes dismissive, which is easily interpreted as rudeness by buyers. This is not to excuse such lack of service—it is inexcusable. But the explanation can at least help you understand where the officer is coming from. And you may want to take your business elsewhere.

- *There are mistakes on my preliminary closing statement or on my final closing statement or both.* This is the reason you need to check everything, including the math. Even though the escrow officer handling your deal may seem smug and superconfident, don't assume the paperwork was done correctly. Just hitting one wrong key on a computer keypad can cost you thousands. And it's very difficult to correct after escrow has closed.

- *The charges are excessive, much higher than I was led to believe they would be when I opened escrow.* This is more often the case with small companies than large ones because the large companies often have posted prices. It's usually too late to complain when escrow is about to close. You need to comparison shop before you open escrow.

Have I asked people I trust to recommend a particular company?

You can simply pick up the Yellow Pages of the phone book and look for escrow–title insurance companies. If you're living in a large metropolitan area, there will probably be dozens of them. In addition, most large real estate companies operate their own escrow companies and are affiliated with title companies. However, as with most services, you are far better off if you can get a recommendation from someone you trust. Perhaps it's a trusted friend, relative, or associate who recently closed a deal on a home and was very impressed with the service they received and the price they were charged.

Am I giving into demands by the seller or the agent to use an escrow–title insurance company of their choosing?

☐

If you're paying for escrow and title insurance services, and you usually are, you should be able to choose the company you want. Sometimes sellers will write into your purchase agreement that the sale is subject to using a specific title insurance company. This could be illegal—the seller may not require, as a condition of sale, the use of a specific title company. (Technically, a violation may entitle you to compensation up to three times the cost of the title company fee.) Additionally, an agent may not normally require that you use a particular escrow–title insurance company. The agent should also disclose if there is a financial arrangement between the agency and the escrow–title insurance company (this arrangement is called a *controlled,* or *affiliated, business interest*). A lender may require you to use a particular escrow–title insurance company as a condition of getting financing provided that there is no financial arrangement between the lender and that escrow–title insurance company.

Have I compared prices and services?

☐

You don't have to show up at the doorstep of every escrow–title insurance company to comparison shop. Just use the phone. Call up and ask to talk to the office manager. Explain that you're purchasing a home and want to open an escrow account and get title insurance. Give the pertinent details, such as the price and the kind of financing, and ask for a quote. Usually it will happily be given, although it may be in the form of a range of prices depending on services performed. Or in some states it will be a set or regulated fee. Typically the price is based on the sales price of the property. The higher the sales price, the higher the charge for escrow and title insurance services. Once you've picked the company you want, then go to their officers in person and get a written statement of what your costs will be. You need to have something in writing just in case the prices mushroom upward when escrow is ready to close.

QUESTIONS TO ASK THE ESCROW–TITLE INSURANCE COMPANY

What is your full charge?

Usually title insurance companies will have a set fee that they charge for insurance based on the type of title policy you get. So when you ask about their charges for their services, they simply go down a chart to the purchase price, read across, and that's the fee. Be sure to ask if there's a separate charge for an *abstract of title,* which will tell you if there are any problems with the title. Often the abstract is included in the insurance fee. (The title company has to do the abstract anyhow as part of the insuring procedure.) Ask the escrow company what their fee is. Be sure to also ask if their fee covers *all* services, or if there will be extra fees for extra services. Sometimes the extras will be nothing more than garbage fees used to bump up the price. And sometimes these garbage fees can total more than the basic escrow charge, which you will also be asked to pay. Try to get it all in writing so that there won't be any confusion or "ups" at closing. Recheck Chapter 3 for limitations on charges.

What will your services cover?

You don't just want the cheapest price. You want the best price for the services that you need. If you know them, describe carefully all of the services you may need. If your purchase is contingent upon the sale of your old home, for example, you may actually need two separate escrow accounts. Find out what you'll be charged for both, or if they can be combined into one. Sometimes an escrow company will cut you a deal if you're bringing in more business. Be sure to ask your agent for help here.

Will there be an additional charge for a lender's escrow?

Some lenders will require that you run a separate escrow for the financing. Find out if there will be an additional cost for this (there usually is). Try to negotiate the cost down. Remember, everything in real estate is negotiable, including escrow fees. Contact the lender. Sometimes it can negotiate this fee down if it does a lot of business with the escrow company.

Will I be charged if the deal falls through?

This can be a big charge, and most buyers fail to ask about it. Opening escrow is simple. You just walk in and hand over your purchase agreement. The escrow officer says he or she will take care of it. Within a few days (or sometimes within hours or even minutes), the officer will present you with preliminary escrow instructions, which you'll be asked to sign. Read the fine print carefully. It may include a paragraph stating that if the deal falls through, you're still obliged to pay for the escrow services. That means that, even through no fault of your own, if the sellers can't go through with the deal and you've got no home to purchase, you could owe thousands of dollars to the escrow company! Usually the fee for a blown deal is considerably less than it is for a completed deal. Nevertheless, it's money you won't want to pay. Try to negotiate that clause out of the papers you sign. Often if your real estate agent does a lot of business with the escrow company, he or she can get it taken out. Or the lender might be able to do so. If it is left in the agreement and the deal doesn't go through, expect to be charged at least something for escrow services.

Will you give me a discount?

Surprisingly, title insurance companies often will. If the property you are buying was sold in the previous 3 years through the same title company, the work that needs to be done is greatly reduced. After all, the title company would need to go back only 3 years to reach its own original records. Why shouldn't it cut you a deal in these circumstances? Title companies may reduce their premiums by 25 percent or more as a reissue because of this "repeat business." However, they're unlikely to do it unless you ask. This is one reason you may want to ask the sellers when they purchased the home you are buying. If it was within the last few years, you may want to ask them which title company they used. Then you can go there and try to negotiate a lower price. (If the sellers are splitting the title insurance cost with you, they should be more than happy to go along with this.)

Is there a separate charge for an abstract of title?

As noted above, the title company has to complete an abstract of title as part of the process of searching the title in order to give insurance. The abstract is done as soon as the escrow account is opened. At the close of escrow, the title company goes back to verify the abstract and then just checks for the time period between the date the abstract was made and the date title is to be recorded. If there has been no new action on the title, it records the deed in your name. (Recording is usually done either at the last or first moment of the day so that no new items affecting title can be sneaked in.) Generally, there is not a separate charge for the abstract research and preparation. However, there can be a charge *if* you don't close escrow. For example, if the deal doesn't go through, even though it's not your fault, the title company may want to charge you for having prepared the abstract. Sometimes this fee is waived for agents or lenders who bring in a lot of business. Check to see if this is the case.

11
Removing Contingencies

QUESTIONS YOU SHOULD ASK YOURSELF

What is a *contingency*?

It is a clause inserted into your real estate offer that makes your purchase contingent on something else. It is also often called a *subject-to clause*. For example, as noted in Chapter 5, you could make your purchase contingent upon the sellers' paying your nonrecurring closing costs (NRCC). If the sellers refuse to pay your closing costs, there is no deal. Even if the sellers agree, there may be a time limit on the contingency—for example, if you can't get financing within 30 days, the deal falls through (and you get your deposit back). There is a wide variety of other common contingency clauses often inserted into real estate purchase offers including the following:

- *Finance contingency.* This makes your purchase contingent upon (or subject to) your getting financing. When you include a specific amount, term, interest rate, and points, you narrow the offer dramatically. For example, you might limit your contingency to a 30-year, fixed-rate mortgage at no more than 6 percent interest and no more than 2 points. If you're unable to get financing at this level or better, there's no deal. Often sellers will insist that you have only 2 weeks or 30 days or whatever to arrange for this financing, thus limiting the time they have their property off the market.

- *Home inspection contingency.* This makes the purchase contingent upon (or subject to) your giving approval to the purchase after a professional home inspection has been conducted. Typically you are given up to 2 weeks for the approval.

- *Disclosure approval.* This contingency establishes a deadline, often a week or less, by which the buyer must agree to move forward with the purchase with the full knowledge of the property disclosures proffered by the sellers. In some states there is an automatic contingency. For example, in California buyers have 3 days after they receive the sellers' disclosures to approve the purchase in light of the disclosures. If you don't approve, then there is no deal.

- *Termite and fungus clearance contingency.* The sellers must provide a state-approved clearance. Sometimes there is a time limit—usually within 30 days of signing the purchase agreement.

- *Fix-up contingency.* If there are physical problems with the property (which may have been revealed in the course of the professional home inspection), the sellers may have a limited time to get them corrected.

- *Sale-of-property contingency.* When real estate isn't moving too quickly, sellers will sometimes accept an offer subject to the sale of your existing home. For example, you may have 30 or 45 days to close the sale of your old home before buying the current one. If you can't sell the old home, then typically you're under no obligation to the buy the new one. In hot markets few sellers will accept such a contingency.

- *Approval contingency.* This clause gives you a few days to get approval for the purchase from someone who has a controlling interest in the purchase, typically from relative, trust, or estate that is giving you the money to buy the house. Most sellers won't object if it's just for a day or two. If it's a week or longer, most will not agree.

- *Frivolous contingency.* You can include a subject-to clause based on anything in the purchase

agreement. You can make the sale subject to little
green men from Mars appearing or the ocean
running dry. Or your winning the state lottery.
However, don't expect any competent seller to
accept such stipulations. Extraordinary contingencies usually just nix the deal.

- *Other contingencies.* There also is a host of other
  common contingencies that can be inserted in
  the fine print (boilerplate) of the purchase agreement. They involve such things as the sale being
  subject to the sellers' being able to offer clear
  title, the house appraisal coming in at an appropriate amount, or there being no problems with
  the city or county.

How do the contingencies factor into the closing process?

Many real estate agents describe the closing process as a
matter of removing contingencies one at a time until you,
the buyer, are fully committed to making the purchase.
Only at that time can the escrow close. Usually there is a
time limit and some action required to remove each contingency. For example, you must apply for and obtain
financing to remove the financing contingency. You must
contract with a professional home inspector, get the property inspected, and approve the report in order to remove
the inspection contingency. And so on. Each time a contingency is removed, the paperwork verifying that fact is
forwarded to the escrow holder, which accepts and holds
it. When all the contingencies have been satisfied, the
escrow holder usually calls for funds, and the closing is
completed. *Note:* As each contingency is removed, your
ability to gracefully get out of the deal is reduced a bit
more.

Do I really need contingencies in my offer?

Contingencies offer you protection. Consider, for example, if you did *not* have a finance contingency in your
offer and, for whatever reason, you couldn't get a loan to
buy the property. Without a contingency clause to protect
you in that event, you would be committed to going
through with the deal. Without financing, however, you'd

probably be incapable of moving forward. Then the sellers could claim your deposit and potentially even sue
your for specific performance (trying to force you to go
through with the deal). All because you didn't have a
finance contingency. With a contingency clause in place,
however, you normally show that you can't get the loan,
you get your deposit back, and you're on your way. Without a home inspection contingency, you probably would
have to take the home as is, without having the opportunity to have it inspected or approve the inspection. In
very hot markets with multiple offers, some daredevil
buyers will make noncontingent offers in the hopes of
getting the sellers to accept their offer over others'. This is
the riskiest of ploys because these buyers have little protection if things don't go their way or if the property turns
out to have unforeseen problems.

Will it weaken my offer?

Every contingency you add to your offer weakens it in the
eyes of the sellers. They would prefer an offer with no
contingencies. That way they would be assured that the
property was sold when they signed (or at the least, they
would get the deposit). With contingencies, as noted
above, the sale really isn't complete until weeks after they
sign, when all of the contingencies are removed. Buying a
property often comes down to adding enough contingencies to protect yourself, while leaving out as many as possible in order to entice the sellers to sign.

Am I giving myself enough time?

When you insert a contingency into your purchase offer,
you should always give yourself enough time to see it
through. For example, a home inspection contingency is
typically for 2 weeks. On a conventional tract house, that
should be plenty of time to get a professional inspector
out to take a look at the property. But what if it's an older
home that will require more rigorous inspections of its
roof, heating, plumbing, and electrical systems? Will you
need 3 or 4 weeks? Some agents suggest you put in the
amount of time you'll really need. Others suggest just
putting in the conventional 2 weeks and then, if something develops in the basic report, asking for more time.

The theory here is that the sellers are more likely to extend the time once they've already agreed to the sale than they are likely to agree to a longer time before they sign. This also applies to other contingencies. For example, is 2 weeks enough time for you to secure financing? Is 30 days? Or even 45? Be sure that you carefully consider any time constraints that you agree to as part of your contingencies.

Is it realistic?

Sometimes contingencies are unrealistic and are better left out of the purchase agreement. For example, you may be worried that your closing costs will be exorbitant. So you put a clause into the purchase agreement specifying that the sale is subject to your closing costs not being more than $3000. When sellers look at this offer, what are they to think? They will probably automatically figure that your closing costs will be more than $3000 and if you're not going to pay them, who is? The answer is: the sellers! (The only other party to the deal would be the agent, and if you expect the agent to cough up part of his or her commission for your closing costs, you'd better be negotiating that well in advance!) The point here is that you must be realistic about your contingencies *if* you want to get the deal signed by the sellers.

Who should write the contingency?

It's important to understand that real estate offers are intended to be legally binding contracts. Once you and the sellers sign, both are supposed to be on the hook. In your case, if you fail to live up to the terms of the offer, you could lose the deal and the deposit. And in a worst-case scenario, you could end up in a lawsuit with the sellers. All this could happen *if* one or more of your contingencies were written improperly. (For example, the person who wrote your finance contingency did it in such a way as to not protect you in case you didn't get your needed financing.) Therefore, it is imperative that the contingency clauses be written correctly.

Almost all modern real estate purchase offers are multiple pages long and are created by attorneys. Very often most of the contingencies that you will want are already included. All that's necessary is to check off the appropriate ones. You will want to have your real estate agent assist you with this. On the other hand, if you need to insert an uncommon contingency that's not already part of the document, it will have to be written from scratch. In this case you'll want to have a competent real estate attorney do it for you. Unless you're very savvy in real estate, don't try writing contingencies into an offer yourself. Unless your real estate agent is also very savvy and experienced, don't have him or her write them in. This is a case in which paying an attorney to do the job is money well spent. (It's also a good idea to have your attorney check over the whole document, just in case.)

QUESTIONS TO ASK YOUR ESCROW HOLDER OR AGENT

What must I do to remove a contingency?

Today's closings mostly involve removing contingencies. Once you and the sellers have signed off, you'll want to immediately get started. You should ask both your agent and your escrow holder what you should be doing to remove the contingencies. In some cases the agent will be doing some of the work; for example, arranging for a termite clearance or a home inspection. In other cases the escrow holder will be doing the work; for example, arranging for an abstract of title and calling for payoffs on the existing financing. However, in most cases your big job will be to go out there and quickly get the financing you need within the time frame of your finance contingency. In addition, there might be some other contingency that's part of your agreement that you should also be working on. For example, you may need to facilitate the sale of your existing home if you have a sale contingency. Your agent and escrow holder should be able to tell you where to get started.

How do I accomplish it?

Removing contingencies can sometimes be easy, other times difficult. For example, to remove the financing contingency, you need to find a lender, fill out an application, and provide the necessary documentation, such as 1040s, old wage slips, or whatever. Without complications, it may be only an hour's worth of work. Or you may want to crawl under the house and into the attic with the home inspector to see just what you're getting. You may want to study the inspection report and disclaimers and take them to your attorney, agent, builder, and trusted friend for their opinions. It could take you days to accomplish removing the contingencies that apply to you. Be sure to check with your agent, your escrow holder, and even your lawyer to find out just what you need do. And make sure you get started right away.

What is *constructive* versus *active notice?*

Your approval of such things as a home inspection report and other contingencies can be given one of two ways, and usually your purchase agreement will specify which way. *Active approval* simply means that you must sign a document giving your approval by the deadline. If you fail to sign that approval document by the specified date, you haven't given your approval and, depending on the contingency, the deal could fall through. *Constructive approval* usually means that if you don't actively disapprove of the report within the time frame, it is assumed that you do approve of it. Note that in the case of active approval, you must actively sign that you approve; otherwise, it is assumed that you do not approve. In the case of constructive approval, you must actively sign that you disapprove; otherwise, it is assumed that you *do* approve. Be sure that you understand how your approval is to be given and act accordingly. You don't want to miss out simply because you don't properly understand the terms of your contract. Check with your agent and/or attorney to be sure.

Which contingencies need be removed first?

Since contingencies usually have a time frame, you want to immediately get started working on those that will take the longest. That usually means the financing. However, others could take priority as well. For example, if there's a problem with the house, you may need not only to get a professional inspector but also a second opinion from a specialist such as a soils engineer (for ground movement problems) or a structural engineer (for cracks in the home). If you have to squeeze all this into a 14-day approval time frame, you'll need to get cracking. As suggested, however, your first course of action is to determine what will take the longest and move forward with it. Sometimes you must work on all the contingencies at the same time!

Do I really want to remove the contingency?

Remember, if you or your agent and/or attorney wrote the contingency into the offer, it probably is there to protect you. You want to remove it only when you no longer need the protection. For example, you'll want to remove the financing contingency only after you're sure you can get financing. You'll want to remove the sellers' disclaimer contingency only after you've read and approved their disclaimers. While you need to be in a hurry to get the closing done, you don't want to be in so much of a hurry that you remove your protections too soon.

Can the time frame be extended?

Yes, almost any time frame for fulfilling a contingency can be extended. However, it normally requires that both you and the sellers agree to the time extension, and that's the rub. If you need just a few more days to solve a financing problem, for example, most sellers will go along. It's a lot easier for them to wait a bit longer than to put the home back on the market and try to find a new buyer. On the other hand, if it's a really hot market and there's another buyer with a higher offer waiting in the wings, don't expect those sellers to cut you any slack.

12
Signing the Right Documents at Closing

QUESTIONS TO ASK YOURSELF

Should I sign?

Whenever I'm faced with signing a lot of documents, I always remember the rule of thumb that an attorney once told me: Your signature rarely protects you; it usually protects the other person. At the closing of escrow, you'll be asked to sign a host of documents, almost all of them from the lender. Usually the only way you can get the loan will be to sign all of them without making any changes. You'll also be asked to sign the closing escrow instructions and to come up with the money for the down payment and your share of the closing costs. (Since it may take a while for your check to clear, you may have been asked to deposit this money a day or so earlier.) My recommendation is that you sign only if you thoroughly understand what you're signing, you have been competently advised that everything is in order, and you feel it's the right thing to do.

What will happen if I don't sign?

Assuming there's no error or mistake on the part of the lender, not signing the documents means you won't get the mortgage, and, presumably, the deal won't close. Further, you may get billed a charge from the lender or the mortgage broker, depending on what your original agreement with them was. The seller could get angry and

153

could demand your deposit. The seller could even sue you for specific performance. The escrow holder might want to charge you for services performed, even though the deal did not close. You could be liable for fees to a home inspector, termite clearance company, and others whose services you contracted for. All of which is to say, if you decide not to sign at closing, you'd better have a very good reason.

What if there's an error in the documents or the charges are excessive?

An error is usually a good reason for not signing. If the escrow holder made it (incorrectly added figures, for example), have him or her correct it. Once errors are pointed out, the escrow officer is usually very fast to make corrections. If the lender made it (the wrong mortgage amount or interest rate, for example), be sure to immediately contact the lender about a correction. Chances are a whole new set of lender's closing documents will need to be drawn. On the other hand, if there are unexpected or excessive charges, you may be on the hook. Compare the charges you received with the estimates on the good-faith estimate you were given at the time you applied for the mortgage. Complain loudly about any major increases. If your lender guaranteed to not increase fees, complain even louder. Get your attorney involved. Keep in mind, however, that if the lender refuses to budge and you need to close the loan, you may need to sign in order to save the deal (see above). The best time to argue with the lender is when you apply for the mortgage, not when you're ready to close escrow.

Can I get advice from the escrow officer?

Probably not. In the old days, going back decades, escrow officers used to be very forthcoming in offering helpful advice and suggestions. However, with our increasingly litigious society, escrow holders are now usually advised by their attorneys not to offer any advice at all. And most won't. They'll tell you where to sign. They'll explain what the documents are—for example, "These are the papers that your lender wants you to sign." Or, "This is an identification sheet describing who you are." But ask them whether or not you should sign, and you'll undoubtedly draw a blank.

Should I have my attorney present?

Yes, this is definitely a good idea. Unfortunately, most people who close on homes don't have their attorney present to represent them. Thus, they show up and sign a whole series of documents, and they do not know what they are signing or what the consequences of their signature on the paper will be. Having your own attorney at a closing is invaluable because he or she can explain the consequences to you of signing (as well as of not signing). Further, the attorney can check the documents to see that they were correctly prepared.

Should I have my real estate agent present?

Yes. Often, particularly if your agent has been in the business a long time, he or she can most clearly explain the documents you are being asked to sign. However, keep in mind that most real estate agents are not attorneys. And agents who are not also attorneys are not supposed to give any legal advice. Further, for fear of lawsuits, many agents today will simply refuse to show up at the closing. They are afraid that they will say something that will later be held against them.

In what form should my payment be?

Your money (the remainder of the down payment after the deposit as well as the closing costs) should be in the safest form possible, after cash. A bank check could do, but it might take 2 weeks or more to fully clear, so most escrow holders find it unacceptable. A cashier's check is better, but today these also may take several days to clear. (Surprising to most people, a cashier's check can sometimes be canceled or the money behind it withdrawn so the bank won't honor it, hence the delays.) Probably the fastest is a wire transfer, which can be done almost instantaneously. However, be sure you understand how it's handled, and use all appropriate security measures to be sure the money isn't accidentally or fraudulently transferred elsewhere. While cash is fast, it is also the most insecure (robbery with big sums is always a possibility), and so it should probably not be used.

QUESTIONS TO ASK THE ESCROW HOLDER

Are all the documents ready?

You should call the escrow officer before going down to his or her office to determine that everything is ready for you. You don't want to waste your time making more than one trip. And signing in advance rarely helps you out. When everything is ready for you, the escrow officer will let you know. Then you, and your spouse if you have one, can go to his or her office and sign the papers all at once. Be prepared to spend about an hour, at minimum.

When will the loan be funded?

Just because you sign the loan documents doesn't mean the escrow will immediately close. First, your lender must send the funds to escrow. Your escrow officer probably has already called for funds (or will shortly) and should be able to report back to you when the lender says the money will be there. Usually it's a matter of no more than a day or so. Sometimes, however, the lender itself can be short, and there could be a delay. Since this could adversely affect the deal, you will want to immediately contact the lender and do everything you can to speed things up. On occasion, lenders have been known to not fund through no fault of the buyer's. They simply experience their own financial problems. In that case, to save the deal, you would have to immediately run out and as quickly as possible secure other financing.

When will the escrow close?

Closings occur typically at the end of the day the loan is funded or the next morning. Your escrow officer should be able to give you a precise time. It's important that this be specified because usually your getting possession of the property is tied to the escrow closing. Keep in mind that sometimes this can be inadvertently delayed a day or two due to a heavy load of closings. If it's any longer, immediately go back to the escrow holder and demand to know what the problem is and when the escrow will close. Your attorney and agent should be able to help you bring pressure here. Once the escrow is complete or perfect (everything necessary is there including all funds), not closing can become a very serious matter with legal repercussions for the escrow holder.

Is there anything else I need to do?

If there is, the escrow holder probably will tell you. But it doesn't hurt to ask anyhow. There may be some document that the lender needs from you. Or some release you need to get from someone else. Don't let escrow hang up because you weren't aware of something you needed to do to facilitate closing.

QUESTIONS TO ASK YOUR ATTORNEY

Should I sign all the documents?

Providing you with the answer to that question is what your lawyer is getting paid the big bucks for. A simple yes or no will do. Some, however, will hem and haw and try to throw it back on you without giving a clear opinion. For example, I've heard an attorney say, "You can sign if you feel you want to go through with this purchase and if you feel the lender, seller, and escrow have prepared the documents correctly." That's not good enough. You want to know that the lender's documents are correct, necessary, in order, and will not harm you. The same goes for any documents from the sellers and escrow holder. You are paying for legal advice from an attorney, and you should get it.

Does anything need to be modified before I sign?

Be careful here. If a particular document was prepared incorrectly and your attorney says you shouldn't sign until it's modified or corrected, then you should probably follow his or her advice. Many attorneys, however, love to modify documents so they favor you more than the other party. Give some attorneys an opportunity and they will begin changing everything. However, that seldom works when dealing with a lender. Lenders have their own attorneys, and if you don't sign exactly as they've prepared the loan documents, for example, they won't loan you the money. Follow your attorney's advice. But also use common sense.

What are the consequences of signing?

This goes along with explaining what the documents are that you're being asked to sign. Your attorney should carefully tell you that, for example, signing an addendum makes it part of the original agreement to which it's added or that there are steep penalties for lying on the loan application, and so on.

What are the consequences of not signing?

If your attorney advised you not to sign, he or she should also let you know the possible consequences of that action, which might be serious such as losing your deposit or having the seller sue you for specific performance.

13
Extras! Extras!

QUESTIONS TO ASK YOURSELF

What are *extra costs*?

These are closing costs that you usually discover have
been added to your charges at closing. They are often
unanticipated. An extra charge could be a commission to
your buyer's agent or a transaction fee or something else.
However, they are not garbage fees in the sense that they
are not being added in to pad or increase the costs to you
for a service. (An example of a garbage fee is an increase
in a lender's fee that the lender had added not to be compensated for additional services he or she performed but
just to pad an existing fee. Lenders sometimes increase
fees to increase their yield.) Rather, these are charges from
unexpected sources that you are being asked to pay. The
big question you should ask yourself about such charges
is, "Did someone tell me that I was going to have to pay
this fee? Did I forget about it?" Sometimes, with the
excitement of purchasing a house and with all of the
many things involved in closing an escrow, you may have
simply overlooked these. Before making a challenge (or at
least a vociferous one!), play back your memory to see if
you didn't actually agree to the charge at some earlier
date. It could save a lot of hassle, and potentially some
embarrassment.

Do I have to pay them?

It depends on what the extra charges are and whether
or not you agreed to pay them. A lot depends on what
you signed. Remember, your signature probably protects

159

others more than it protects you. If one of those myriad documents you signed was an agreement to pay for an extra, you're probably on the hook. On the other hand, if you gave your verbal okay, then you probably should pay it, but you may not be bound to. Here, it could be a matter more of conscience than of legality, although in some cases you can be held to a verbal agreement. On the other hand, if you never agreed to pay the extra charge, or what's worse, specifically said (or wrote) that you wouldn't, then it's time to fight it tooth and nail. Remember, the final closing statement should reflect the preliminary closing statement that you signed and that was based on the purchase agreement. Go back to the original documents. If you haven't agreed to it, challenge its inclusion by the escrow holder.

QUESTIONS TO ASK YOUR AGENT

Why am I being charged a commission?

Normally the buyer expects the sellers to pay for the real estate commission. If they listed the house, then presumably, the commission is their responsibility. There are, however, some exceptions. If, as part of the purchase agreement, the buyer agreed to pay part or all of the sellers' closing costs (including commission), then it will appear on the buyer's closing statement. This sometimes happens in a very hot market where there are multiple offers and, in order to be the winning bidder, the buyer goes to extreme lengths. If you did this, then you can expect to pay. The other possibility is that you were using a "buyer's agent." Here, you sort of "list" yourself with an agent, hiring him or her to find just the right house for you. Usually buyers' agents will have you sign an agreement that may specify that if they find you a house, you owe them a commission. You have to be very careful about the agreement you sign. It should say that the agent's first recourse is to try to split the commission with the selling agent, which often can be done. However, if it can't be done, or you agreed to pay the agent a commission regardless, then you're probably on the hook. Barring these two exceptions, it's probably an error (the charge should be the sellers), and you should bring it to the escrow holder's attention. *Note:* Normally an agency agreement must be in writing for an agent to win a breach of contract lawsuit.

What is an *agency* or *transaction fee*?

This is something relatively new that has come about because of the highly competitive nature of real estate today. Agents, probably the one you are dealing with, work for brokers who run offices. However, for the brokers to get the very best agents, they must give them a highly one-sided split. The typical split for a run-of-the-mill agent is 50-50. The agent gets half of whatever he or she earns, and the office gets half. With a "superagent," one who brings in a lot of deals, the split is more like 80-20 or even 90-10. The agent gets 80 to 90 percent of the commission, and the office gets 10 or 20 percent. Since these superagents often bring in three-quarters of all business, the real estate offices have found themselves in a situation in which they simply aren't getting enough money to run their operation and make a profit. Hence, rather than reduce the fees paid to agents (which means the agents might leave and go elsewhere), they've taken to charging buyers and sellers additional fees. These have names such as an "agency fee" or a "transaction fee." They can be anywhere from a few hundred dollars to a thousand dollars or more.

Do I have to pay an agency or transaction fee?

You might. Sellers, for example, often don't realize that they agree to pay such a fee when they sign their listing agreement. It might be in the "small print." However, if they agreed to it in writing and the agent did produce a buyer ready, willing, and able to purchase, then presumably they will have to pay the fee. Or fight it. Assuming you, as a buyer, didn't sign any agency agreement (for a buyer's agent, for example—see above), then the only other time you were likely to have signed it was in the preliminary closing statement. Go back and check. Was it there in the fine print? (See Chapter 3.) If so, you, too, may be on the hook. Remember, if you actually owe the fee yet refuse to sign and close the deal, you'll have an angry seller to deal with. On the other hand, if you never agreed to this fee and it just suddenly appeared, I'd certainly demand its removal. Even if the agent complains that he or she will have to pay it to his or her broker if you don't pay it, I'd still demand its removal. You shouldn't have to pay for anything you didn't agree to. If you have trouble with having the agency or transaction fee removed, it might a very good time to check with your attorney.

What about hollering?

No agent wants an angry client. An angry client tells his or her friends, relatives, the local newspaper, and anyone who'll listen that he or she has been ripped off. If you honestly feel you were cheated, then tell your agent about it in no uncertain terms. No, you don't need to actually raise your voice. But it wouldn't hurt to make your feelings profoundly known. And if you bring your attorney with you, it can make an even bigger impression.

Will you remove it?

The agent isn't likely to remove a commission charge if you've previously agreed to pay it in writing. (It must be in writing to be enforceable in most states.) On the other hand, if it was a verbal agreement, then it's certainly open to challenge. Go to the agent's broker. Speak to the local real estate board. If you challenge it and the agent doesn't have a legal leg to stand on, he or she can be expected to remove it.

What is a *home warranty plan?*

This can be an unexpected extra. It is an insurance policy that covers the systems of the home you are buying such as plumbing, electrical, and heating. With extensions it can even cover the roof, the pool and spa, and other areas. Generally it begins once you move in (although some plans can begin as soon as the home is listed). If you have a problem that's covered, you call a special number, and a service technician is sent out to correct the problem. Typically regardless of the cost to fix it, your cost is limited to a small amount, say, $35 or $50. However, sometimes the plan limits the total amount that is covered. For example, heating systems may be limited to $500 or $1000. Roofs can likewise be limited. The cost of the plan is generally between $250 to $500 depending on what's covered and who's administering it. Usually the sellers pay for it.

How come the sellers aren't being charged for it?

In most transactions, the sellers pay the premium for a home warranty plan. It's part of their guarantee that you're getting a home in good condition. This way, if something goes wrong, they won't be hearing from you— the plan will take care of the problem. For the agents, it's good business. This way the agent doesn't hear from you either. Most agents encourage their sellers to take out a home warranty plan for the buyer. However, there's no rule that says the seller must pay for the plan. It all depends on what you agreed to in the purchase agreement and in the preliminary closing statement. If you agreed to it, you'll get the bill and probably will have to pay for it. (See also Chapter 6.)

QUESTIONS TO ASK YOUR ESCROW HOLDER

Who authorized these extras to be charged to me?

The answer should be that the escrow officer is merely following the preliminary escrow instructions, which you already agreed to by signing them. Go back and check them out. Did the escrow officer make a mistake? Or did you actually agree to this? If it's a mistake, demand that it be corrected. If you agreed to it, then you might be on the hook. Go back to the purchase agreement to see what was originally agreed upon. If these costs cannot be traced to the purchase agreement, and if the escrow officer says that the seller or the agent or someone else instructed him or her to add the costs to your closing instructions and statement, then you can demand they be removed. The escrow documents constitute an agreement between you and the seller based on the seller's and your instructions. No one except you and the seller by common agreement should be able to amend them once they've been signed. (Of course, hopefully you caught this in the preliminary instructions.)

How do I get them removed?

If you have a quarrel with the escrow officer over an extra fee, the best thing to do is to ask how to get it removed. You may need to check with the seller, the agent, your attorney, or even the escrow holder's superior. You may learn that the fee is legitimate and you must pay it. Or you may find that with a little persuasion aimed at the right person, it simply disappears.

14
Using the Final Walk-Through Inspection

QUESTIONS TO ASK YOURSELF

What is the *final walk-through inspection?*

This is your last chance to inspect and approve the property before the escrow closes. It involves your walking through the home just as you did when you first checked out the property. What you are looking for is anything different from what it was when you first saw it. The house should be exactly the same, unless the sellers have already moved out. Even in that case, however, the only difference would be that the furnishings would be gone. In order to have the right to a final walk-through, it must be specified in your purchase agreement as a condition of sale. (See Chapter 6.)

If the sellers have moved, will it make a big difference?

Yes, dramatically so. Be prepared for numerous scuff marks everywhere and especially in places where furniture was located and where carpets were. Usually such scuff marks amount to just normal wear and tear, and they don't show up until all of the sellers' furnishings are out of the home. Seeing the scuff marks often makes a convincing argument for repainting before you move in, but the marks are not usually something you can ding the sellers for. However, if anything you thought went with the house is missing (such as a chandelier, stove, carpeting, or draperies) or if there is extensive damage, such as holes in the wall, it's time to raise a ruckus—see below. *Note:* You can expect the sellers to give you the place *broom swept clean.* That is usually not nearly clean enough for most buyers. Thus, you may want to call in a professional cleaning service, at your own expense.

When should I have the final walk-through inspection?

You want to schedule it before the close of escrow but as close to it as is practical. Typically it's done a day or two before the closing. The reasoning here is that this way you can see any changes or damage to the property made by the sellers. On the other hand, it's close enough to the closing that, presumably, the seller won't have time to make any further changes or do any further damage after your inspection and before you gain possession. Don't have the inspection *after* the closing. By then the sale is fait accompli, and there's much less you can do about problems.

Should I take anyone with me?

Yes, take anyone along who saw the property before you made the offer. This person(s) can confirm any concerns about changes or new damage that you may have. Also, be sure your agent goes with you. This person presumably has had experience with final walk-throughs and can reassure you about some of your concerns. For example, if there's a scuff on the wall where a rocking chair once sat, your agent will probably assure you that you didn't see it initially because the chair was there and it's nothing to get upset about. On the other hand, keep in mind that your agent wants to close the deal. If he or she begins pooh-poohing things you're very concerned about, get another opinion, preferably from your attorney.

Do I know what I should look for?

Look for damaged and missing items. Damage includes such things as broken stove, oven, heating system, water pipes, holes in walls or windows (and window screens), and so on. Items missing or changed for items of lower value sometimes include the following:

- Stove
- Oven
- Floor coverings
- Window coverings
- Chandeliers
- Door handles
- Decorative items attached to the home
- Anything else that's different

Note: Your purchase agreement should specify that all of the above items are included in the sale. (See Chapter 6.) Keep in mind that anything you don't discover will be assumed to be okay. That means that it will probably be your responsibility to fix or correct the problem after you move in.

Do I know what to do if something is missing or damaged?

If something is missing or damaged, then you should carefully note exactly what the problem is. You should get your agent to write up the complaint and then present it to the sellers as a demand. For example, there was a beautiful glass chandelier in the entry hall. In fact, you bought the house to get the chandelier. You had your agent include it in the purchase agreement. But now, it's been replaced by a cheap-looking brass and wood chandelier. You want back the chandelier you saw originally. You should make written demand for the chandelier to the seller. In some cases, entire purchases have been held up for days, weeks, or sometimes even lost because of disagreement over personal property.

What about dirt and mess?

The property should be relatively clean. That means that if the sellers have moved out, all their things including boxes, hangers, and everything else should be gone. There should be no debris lying around. On the other hand, if the floor has only been swept and not mopped, there's almost nothing you can do about it. (Unless you had a cleaning contingency inserted into the purchase agreement, which is highly unlikely.) There should be no large mud or paint stains on the walls. But, then again, don't expect them to be perfectly clean. A lot depends on the character of the sellers and how clean they were. Don't expect the house to live up to your standards. You set them now, when you first move in.

Can I use this as an excuse to get out of the purchase?

This is an important question to ask yourself. Sometimes buyers have decided that they really don't want the home anymore. Maybe they simply don't want to move. Or perhaps they've found another more desirable or less expensive home they'd like to buy. Whatever the reason, chances are that by the time escrow is ready to close, all your other options, such as disapproving a home inspection or seller's disclosures or even your financing contingency, have run out. There's no easy way out of the deal. Unless, this buyer hopes, he or she can make up a problem with the final walk-through. If this is your hope and intent, I discourage it. Most final walk-throughs these days are written with a specific clause stating that it cannot be used as a way to get out of the deal. What this usually means is that for you to make a final-inspection challenge, you must, in fact, find something really wrong. For example, if the house burns down by final inspection time, you can fairly well assume you're out of the deal. On the other hand, finding some dirt on the hallway floor isn't going to do it. Your efforts will be rebuffed by the sellers, their agent, and even your agent. If you're not sure, check with your own attorney.

What if I discover something after I close the deal and move in?

Sometimes it's too late. Sometimes not. If it's a serious problem, such as a faulty roof, and it was not disclosed by the sellers yet they should have known about it (they called a roofer four times the previous winter and he told you that when you called him), then you can probably get them to at least fix the roof. You may even be able to get them to put on a new roof. Call your agent and send a demand to the seller. If they don't respond favorably, consider talking to your attorney.

QUESTIONS TO ASK THE SELLER

Have you had any parties here since the offer was made?

This is the single biggest problem area, particularly if you have a long escrow period (over 30 days). Sometimes sellers feel that the minute they sign a sales agreement, they no longer have to take care of the property. I've seen sellers hold wild parties at these homes during which carpeting, paint, light fixtures, and even the pumps in the swimming pool (they were plugged up!) were ruined. Of course, when the final inspection time comes, the sellers attempt to cover up all the damage. Maybe they've at least partly succeeded. But, if you ask them about parties, you may catch them off guard, and they may admit they had romps every weekend since they signed. If so, look more closely. Check under carpets, behind drapes, and move furniture. Find out anything wrong with the property. Remember, anything you don't find will probably be yours to fix after the escrow closes and you take possession. *Note:* Be careful with carpeting—be sure to check it for pet odors, particularly urination, which often cannot be removed and can be eliminated only by the replacement of the carpeting.

Have you removed or changed anything?

If you've noticed something amiss and the sellers are there, ask them about it. Don't wait to make the challenge in writing, although that's something you may want to do. Point out that the door handles in the entryway are now cheap-looking silver and when you first saw the house, they were polished brass. Your agent should be able to back you up. And most sellers will back down. Often it is just embarrassment that gets you back the items that have been switched.

QUESTIONS TO ASK YOUR AGENT

Will you verify that something is damaged or missing?

Agents hate this. It puts them at odds with the sellers and the selling agent. On the other hand, your agent may have a fiduciary responsibility to you, and if something was switched or damaged or taken, the agent needs to back you up. Any good agent will do this, regardless of the problems it causes for him or her. With your agent to back you up and with your making demands, refusing to sign, and threatening to call your attorney, most sellers will back down and replace or fix the problem items.

What will you do about it?

Once your agent agrees that something was switched, taken, or damaged, he or she should prepare a written demand to give to the sellers' agent and the sellers. It should very clearly spell out the item in question. Some agents have forms already prepared by their attorneys that also spell out the consequences for such actions. A forceful agent can often very quickly get the problem remedied. On the other hand, if your agent doesn't act on your behalf, it may be time to consult with your attorney.

Can you use the final walk-through to get me out of the deal?

The proper answer is no. Just as you can't get out of the deal at this point (see above), your agent can't get you out either. On the other hand, I have seen agents browbeat sellers and even other agents to get their clients out of a purchase agreement. (In these cases the agent wanted to sell their clients a different home.) Agents, particularly those who have been in the business for a long time, can do amazing things. It won't hurt to ask. On the other hand, don't be a party to anything that's illegal or unethical. It could come back to haunt you.

QUESTIONS TO ASK YOUR ATTORNEY

Can you persuade a seller to replace items that were switched, taken, or damaged?

Your attorney will undoubtedly want to know just what proof you have of your assertions. Usually it's just what you saw. However, if you have witnesses such as your agent, or even better, other people who went through the house and who are unrelated to you, your case will undoubtedly be stronger. Sometimes just a letter on an attorney's stationary is enough to convince a wayward seller to get back on the straight and narrow.

What can I do later if I find a big problem I missed during the final walk-through inspection?

Your attorney will undoubtedly want you to inform the sellers either directly or through their agent that there's a significant problem with the property. You should emphasize that this problem was discovered after you took possession. If it wasn't in the disclosures but the sellers should have known about it, or if it was purposely concealed, then your attorney may encourage you to pursue the matter through a lawsuit. If you're correct and there's substantial evidence to back you up, the sellers will sometimes agree to a monetary settlement to make the whole thing go away.

15

Finally Taking Possession of Your New Home

QUESTIONS TO ASK YOURSELF

When do I want to take possession of the property?

□

When you actually get possession of the property is determined by agreement with the sellers. It can be any time from the moment the purchase agreement is signed until 6 months or more after escrow closes. However, as a practical matter, it is usually given upon close of escrow. That's the point at which the sellers no longer own the property and your term of ownership begins. However, it may be to your advantage to get possession at a different time, and this can be a negotiating point when making the deal. For example, you may want possession earlier because of a work commitment. *If* the seller is agreeable and the home is empty, you might move in ahead of the close of escrow and pay rent to the sellers. Or the sellers might want to remain in the property after the close of escrow because, for example, they want their children to finish out the school year. It's all a matter of what both of you agree upon. (For possible problems, see the following.)

How will I get possession?

□

Possession is usually evidenced by the sellers' giving up the keys to the property. They usually give it to their agent, who hands it to your agent, who hands it to you. If the agreement is for possession to be given upon the close of escrow, your agent will typically wait until the deed is recorded to hand over the key. (Otherwise, the agent could be liable if, for some reason, the deed was not recorded and you didn't take ownership but got possession.) Although this happens rarely, sometimes the key will be given to the escrow officer to hand over to the buyer. Once you have the key, you "officially" have possession of the property. However, as a security precaution, the first thing you should do is to have a locksmith change the keys or the locks to the property. You never know who might have an old key from delivery people to relatives of the former owners.

Do I want to get possession before the close of escrow?

As noted above, your circumstances may be such that you may want to move in early. You can propose to the sellers that you rent the property during escrow if the home is already empty, or the sellers are moving. If the house is empty, or even if they have to move earlier, they will consider your offer. However, expect most sellers to refuse. The reason is that if for any reason escrow doesn't close (you can't get financing, the house isn't appraised for the amount you need for the mortgage, there's a title problem, and so on), the sellers would no longer have a house ready for sale. Instead, they would have a house with a tenant inside. Then they would have to ask you to leave. For you this is also a problem since it means you will have to make two moves.

Do I want to let sellers remain in possession after the close?

More often than most suppose, sellers want to stay in the property after the close of escrow. The reasons could be children in school, job commitments, illness, or almost anything. They will propose not giving you possession until a far later date. Most agents would advise against your letting them stay, even if they offer to pay a high rent. The reason is that you would then become a landlord, and you might have trouble getting the sellers out later on. If they refuse to move, your only recourse would be an eviction, which could be costly and could take a lot of time. Further, as tenants, they could leave the place a mess. If you do opt to let the sellers remain in possession after you get ownership, be sure they put up a hefty security and cleaning deposit and at least a month's rent in advance. Also, you may want to read up on how to be an effective landlord. (Check out my book *The Landlord's Troubleshooter*, Dearborn, 1998.)

QUESTIONS TO ASK YOUR AGENT

When do the sellers want to give possession?

This question should be asked when you're making your offer (see Chapter 6). Your agent should confer with the sellers and their agent to determine the sellers' preference. Usually it will be at the close of escrow. If it's afterward, read the questions above.

When will you get me the key?

In the best-case scenario, your agent will arrange to pick up the key to the property before escrow closes, and he or she will hold it until the deed is recorded in your name. Then he or she will give it to you. Sometimes agents fall down on this responsibility, and nobody takes care of the key transfer. If that's the case, then you may need to call the sellers' agent or even the sellers to get the key. Really awkward situations arise when there is nobody able or willing to transfer the key and there is no convenient transfer of possession. As a last resort, you may need to see if the home is empty and if it is, after you have title and technical possession, break a window to get in. Check with your attorney, however, before resorting to this.

Understanding the Terminology

If you're just getting introduced to real estate, you'll quickly realize that people in this field have a language all their own. There are points and disclosures and contingencies and dozens of other terms that can make you think people are talking in a foreign language.

Since buying a home is one of the biggest financial decisions in life, it's a good idea to become familiar with the following terms, which are frequently used in real estate. All too often a lack of understanding can result in very real consequences such as confusion and failure to act (or inappropriate action) on an important issue.

Abstract of Title: A written document produced by a title insurance company (in some states an attorney will do it) giving the history of who owned the property from the first owner forward. It also indicates any liens or encumbrances that may affect the title. A lender will not make a loan, nor can a sale normally conclude, until the title to real estate is clear, as evidenced by the abstract.

Acceleration Clause: A clause that "accelerates" the payments in a mortgage, meaning that the entire amount becomes immediately due and payable. Most mortgages contain this clause (which kicks in if, for example, you sell the property).

Adjustable Rate Mortgage (ARM): A mortgage whose interest rate fluctuates according to an index and a margin agreed to in advance by borrower and lender.

Adjustment Date: The day on which an adjustment is made in an adjustable rate mortgage. It may occur monthly, every 6 months, once a year, or as otherwise agreed.

Agent: Any person licensed to sell real estate, whether a broker or a salesperson.

Alienation Clause: A clause in a mortgage specifying that if the property is transferred to another person, the mortgage becomes immediately due and payable. See also *Acceleration Clause.*

ALTA (American Land Title Association): A more complete and extensive policy of title insurance than most title insurance companies offer. It involves a physical inspection and often guarantees the property's boundaries. Lenders often insist on an ALTA policy, with themselves named as beneficiary.

Amortization: The repaying of the mortgage in equal installments. In other words, if the mortgage is for 30 years, you pay in 360 equal installments. (The last payment is often just a few dollars more or less than the rest of the payments have been. This is the opposite of a balloon payment schedule, by which one payment, usually the last one, is considerably larger than the rest.) See *Balloon Payment.*

Annual Percentage Rate (APR): The actual interest rate paid on a loan, including interest, loan fees, and points. The APR is determined by a government formula.

Appraisal: Valuation of a property, usually by a qualified appraiser, as required by most lenders. The amount of the appraisal is the maximum value on which the loan will be based. For example, if the appraisal is $100,000 and the lender loans 80 percent of value, the maximum mortgage will be $80,000.

ASA (American Society of Appraisers): A professional organization of appraisers.

As Is: A property sold without warrantees from the sellers. The sellers are essentially saying that they won't make any repairs.

Assignment of Mortgage: The lender's sale of a mortgage usually without the borrower's permission. For example, you may obtain a mortgage from XYZ Savings and Loan, which then sells the mortgage to Bland Bank. You will get a letter saying that the mortgage was assigned and you are to make your payments to a new entity. The document used between lenders for the transfer is the "assignment of mortgage."

Assumption: The taking over of an existing mortgage. For example, a seller may have an assumable mortgage on a property. When you buy the property, you take over that seller's obligation under the loan. Today most fixed-rate mortgages are not assumable. Most adjustable rate mortgages are assumable, but the borrower must qualify. FHA and VA mortgages may be assumable if certain conditions are met. When you assume the mortgage, you may be personally liable if there is a foreclosure.

Automatic Guarantee: The power assigned to some lenders to guarantee VA loans without first checking with the Veterans Administration. These lenders can often make the loans more quickly.

Backup: An offer that comes in after an earlier offer is accepted. If both buyer and seller agree, the backup assumes a secondary position to be acted on only if the original deal does not go through.

Balloon Payment: A single mortgage payment, usually the last, that is larger than all the others. In the case of second mortgages held by sellers, often only interest is paid until the due date—then the entire amount borrowed (the principal) is due. See *Second Mortgage*.

Biweekly Mortgage: A mortgage that is paid every other week instead of monthly. Since there are 52 weeks in the year, you end up making 26 payments, or the equivalent of 1 month's extra payment. The additional payments, applied to the principal, significantly reduce the amount of interest charged on the mortgage and often reduce the term of the loan.

Blanket Mortgage: A mortgage that covers several properties instead of a single property. It is used most frequently by developers and builders.

Broker: An independent licensed agent, one who can establish his or her own office. Salespeople, although they are licensed, must work for brokers, typically for a few years, to get enough experience to become fully licensed as independent brokers.

Buydown Mortgage: A mortgage with a lower-than-market interest rate, either for the entire term of the mortgage or for a set period at the beginning—say, 2 years. The buydown is made possible by the builder or seller paying an up-front fee to the lender.

Buyer's Agent: A real estate agent whose loyalty is to the buyer and not to the seller. Such agents are becoming increasingly common today.

Call Provision: A clause in a mortgage allowing the lender to call in the entire unpaid balance of the loan providing certain events have occurred, such as sale of the property. See also *Acceleration Clause.*

Canvass: To work a neighborhood; to go through it and knock on every door. Agents canvass to find listings. Investors and home buyers do it to find potential sellers who have not yet listed their property—and may agree to sell quickly for less.

Caps: Limits put on an adjustable rate mortgage. The interest rate, the monthly payment, or both may be capped.

CC&Rs (Covenants, Conditions, and Restrictions): Limits on the types of activities you as a property owner may engage in on the property. For example, you may be required to seek approval of a home owners' association before adding on to your home or changing the color of the exterior. Or you may be restricted from adding a second or third story to your home.

Certificate of Reasonable Value (CRV): A document issued by the Veterans Administration establishing what the VA feels is the property's maximum value. In some cases, if a buyer pays more than this amount for the property, he or she will not get a VA loan.

Chain of Title: The history of ownership of the property. The title to property forms a chain going back to the first owners. In the Southwest, for example, the chain may start from the original Spanish land grants.

Closing: A meeting at which the seller conveys the title to the buyer and the buyer makes full payment to the seller, including financing, for the property. At the closing, all required documents are signed and delivered, and funds are disbursed. It also refers to the entire process of concluding a purchase.

Commission: The fee charged for an agent's services. Usually, but not always, the seller pays. There is no set fee; rather, the amount is fully negotiable.

Commitment: A promise from the lender to the borrower offering a mortgage at a set amount, interest rate, and cost. Typically, commitments have a time limit—for example, they are good for 5 or 15 days. Some lenders charge for making a commitment if you don't subsequently take out the mortgage (since they have tied up the money for that amount of time). When the lender's offer is in writing, it is sometimes called a *firm commitment.*

Conforming Loan: A mortgage that complies fully with the underwriting requirements of Fannie Mae or Freddie Mac.

Construction Loan: A mortgage made for the purpose of constructing a building. The loan is written for a short term, typically under 12 months, and it is usually paid in installments directly to the builder as the work is completed. Most often, it is an interest-only loan.

Contingency: A condition that limits a contract. For example, the most common contingency says that a buyer is not required to complete a purchase if he or she fails to get necessary financing. See also *Subject To.*

Conventional Loan: Any loan that is not guaranteed or insured by the government.

Convertible Mortgage: An adjustable rate mortgage (ARM) with a clause allowing it to be converted to a fixed-rate mortgage at some time in the future. You may have to pay an additional cost to obtain this type of mortgage.

Cosigner: Someone with better credit (usually a close relative) who agrees to sign your loan if by yourself you do not have a credit rating high enough to qualify for a mortgage. The cosigner is equally responsible for repayment of the loan. (If you don't pay it back, the cosigner may be held liable for the entire balance.)

Credit Report: A report, usually from one of the country's three large credit reporting companies, that gives your credit history. It typically lists all your delinquent payments or failures to pay as well as any bankruptcies and, sometimes, foreclosures. Lenders use the report to determine whether to offer you a mortgage. The fee for obtaining the report is usually under $50, and you are charged for it.

Deal Point: A point on which the deal hinges. It can be as important as the price or as trivial as changing the color of the mailbox.

Deposit: The money that buyers put up (also called *earnest money*) to demonstrate their seriousness in making an offer. The deposit is usually at risk if the buyers fail to complete the transaction and have no acceptable way of backing out of the deal.

Disclosures: A list and explanation of the features and defects in a property that sellers give to buyers. Also a list and explanation of the terms and conditions in a contract such as a mortgage instrument. Most states now require disclosures.

Discount: The amount that a lender withholds from a mortgage to cover the points and fees. For example, you may borrow $100,000, but your points and fees come to $3000; hence the lender will fund only $97,000, discounting the $3000. Also, in the secondary market, a discount is the amount less than face value that a buyer of a mortgage pays in order to be induced to take out the loan. The discount here is calculated on the basis of risk, market rates, interest rate of the note, and other factors. See *Points*.

Dual Agent: An agent who expresses loyalty to both buyers and sellers and agrees to work with both. Only a few agents can successfully play this role.

Due-on-Encumbrance Clause: A little noted and seldom-enforced clause in recent mortgages that allows the lender to foreclose if the borrower gets additional financing. For example, if you secure a second mortgage, the lender of the first mortgage may have grounds for foreclosing. The reasoning here is that if you reduce your equity level by taking out additional financing, the lender may be placed in a less secure position.

Due-on-Sale Clause: A clause in a mortgage specifying that the entire unpaid balance becomes due and payable on sale of the property. See *Acceleration Clause.*

Escrow Company: An independent third party (stakeholder) that handles funds; carries out the instructions of the lender, buyer, and seller in a transaction; and deals with all the documents. In most states, companies are licensed to handle escrows. In some parts of the country, particularly the Northeast, the function of the escrow company may be handled by an attorney.

FHA Loan: A mortgage insured by the Federal Housing Administration. In most cases, the FHA advances no money but instead insures the loan to a lender such as a bank. There is a fee to the borrower, usually paid up front, for this insurance.

Fixed-Rate Mortgage: A mortgage whose interest rate does not fluctuate for the life of the loan.

Fixer-Upper: A home that does not show well and is in bad shape. Often the property is euphemistically referred to in listings as a "TLC" (needs tender loving care) or "handyman's special."

Foreclosure: Legal proceeding in which the lender takes possession and title to a property, usually after the borrower fails to make timely payments on a mortgage.

Fannie Mae: Any of the publicly traded securities collateralized by a pool of mortgages backed by the Federal National Mortgage Association. A secondary lender.

Freddie Mac: A publicly traded security collateralized by a pool of mortgages backed by the Federal Home Loan Mortgage Corporation. A secondary lender.

FSBO: For sale by owner.

Garbage Fees: Extra (and often unnecessary) charges tacked on when a buyer obtains a mortgage.

Graduated-Payment Mortgage: A mortgage whose payments vary over the life of the loan. The payments start out low, then slowly rise until, usually after a few years, they reach a plateau where they remain for the balance of the term. Such a mortgage is particularly useful when you want low initial payments. It is primarily used by first-time buyers, often in combination with a fixed-rate or adjustable rate mortgage.

Growing Equity Mortgage: A rarely used mortgage whose payments increase according to a set schedule. The purpose is to pay additional money into principal and thus pay off the loan earlier and save interest charges.

HOA (Home Owners' Association): An organization found mainly in condominium complexes but also in some single-family areas. It represents homeowners and establishes and maintains neighborhood architectural and other standards. You usually must get permission from the HOA to make significant external changes to your property.

Index: A measurement of an established interest rate used to determine the periodic adjustments for adjustable rate mortgages. There is a wide variety of indexes, including the Treasury bill rates and the cost of funds to lenders.

Inspection: A physical survey of the property to determine if there are any problems or defects.

Jumbo Mortgage: A mortgage for more than the maximum amount of a *Conforming Loan*.

Lien: A claim for money against real estate. For example, if you had work done on your property and refused to pay the worker, he or she might file a *mechanic's lien* against your property. If you didn't pay taxes, the taxing agency might file a *tax lien*. These liens "cloud" the title and usually prevent you from selling the property or refinancing it until they are cleared by paying off the debt.

Loan-to-Value Ratio (LTV): The percentage of the appraised value of a property that a lender will loan. For example, if your property appraises at $100,000 and the lender is willing to loan $80,000, the loan-to-value ratio is 80 percent.

Lock In: To tie up the interest rate for a mortgage in advance of actually getting the loan. For example, a buyer might lock in a mortgage at 7.5 percent so that if rates subsequently rose, he or she would still get that rate. Sometimes there's a fee for this. It's always a good idea to get it in writing from the lender, just to be sure that if rates rise, the lender doesn't change its mind.

Low-Ball: To make a very low initial offer to purchase.

MAI (Member, American Institute of Real Estate Appraisers): An appraiser who has completed rigorous training and has qualified for this title.

Margin: An amount, calculated in points, that a lender adds to an index to determine how much interest you will pay during a period for an adjustable rate mortgage. For example, the index may be at 7 percent, and the margin agreed upon at the time you obtain the mortgage may be 2.7 points. The interest rate for that period, therefore, is 9.7 percent. See also *Index, Points.*

Median Sales Price: The midpoint of the price of homes. As many properties have sold above this price as have sold below it.

MLS (Multiple Listing Service): A service used by Realtors® as a listings exchange. Nearly 90 percent of all homes listed in the country are found on the MLS.

Mortgage: A loan arrangement between a borrower, or *mortgagor,* and a lender, or *mortgagee.* If you don't make your payments on a mortgage, the lender can foreclose, or take ownership of the property, only by going to court. This court action can take a great deal of time, often 6 months or more. Further, even after the lender has taken back the property, you may have an *equity of redemption* that allows you to redeem the property for years afterward, by paying back the mortgage and the lender's costs. The length of time it takes to foreclose, the costs involved, and the equity of redemption make a mortgage much less desirable to lenders than a *Trust Deed.*

Mortgage Banker: A lender that specializes in offering mortgages but none of the other services normally provided by a bank.

Mortgage Broker: A person or company that specializes in providing "retail" mortgages to consumers. It usually represents many different lenders.

Motivated Seller: A seller who has a strong desire to sell. For example, the seller may have been transferred and must move quickly.

Multiple Counteroffers: Comeback offers extended by the seller to several buyers simultaneously.

Multiple Offers: Offers submitted simultaneously from several buyers for the same property.

Negative Amortization: A condition arising when the payment on an adjustable rate mortgage is not sufficiently large to cover the interest charged. The excess interest is then added to the principal, so that the amount borrowed actually increases. The amount that the principal can increase is usually limited to 125 percent of the original mortgage value. Any mortgage that includes payment *Caps* has the potential to be negatively amortized.

Origination Fee: An expense in obtaining a mortgage. Originally, it was a charge that lenders made for preparing and submitting a mortgage. The fee applied only to FHA and VA loans, which had to be submitted to the government for approval. With an FHA loan, the maximum origination fee was 1 percent.

Personal Property: Any property that does not go with the land. Such property includes automobiles, clothing, and most furniture. Some items such as appliances and floor and wall coverings are disputable. See also *Real Property.*

PITI (Principal, Interest, Taxes, and Insurance): These are the major components that go into determining the monthly payment on a mortgage. (Other items include home owners' association dues and utilities.)

Points: A point is 1 percent of a mortgage amount, payable on obtaining the loan. For example, if your mortgage is $100,000 and you are required to pay 2½ points to get it, the charge to you is $2500. Some points may be tax deductible. Check with your accountant. A *basis point* is ¹⁄₁₀₀ of a point. For example, if you are charged ½ point (0.5

percent of the mortgage), the lender may refer to it as "50 basis points."

Preapproval: Formal approval for a mortgage from a lender. You have to submit a standard application and have a credit check. Also, the lender may require proof of income, employment, and money on deposit (to be used for the down payment and closing costs).

Prepayment Penalty: A charge demanded by the lender from the borrower for paying off a mortgage early. In times past (more than 25 years ago), nearly all mortgages carried prepayment penalties. However, those mortgages were also assumable by others. Today virtually no fixed-rate mortgages (other than FHA or VA mortgages) are truly assumable; however some carry a prepayment penalty clause. See *Assumption.*

Private Mortgage Insurance (PMI): Insurance that protects the lender in the event that the borrower defaults on a mortgage. It is written by an independent third-party insurance company and typically covers only the first 20 percent of the lender's potential loss. PMI is normally required on any mortgage that exceeds an 80 percent loan-to-value ratio.

Purchase Money Mortgage: A mortgage obtained as part of the purchase price of a home (usually from the seller) as opposed to a mortgage obtained through refinancing. In some states, no deficiency judgment can be obtained against the borrower of a purchase money mortgage. (That is, if there is a foreclosure and the property brings less than the amount borrowed, the borrower cannot be held liable for the shortfall.)

Real Property: Real estate. This includes the land and anything appurtenant to it, including the house. Certain tests have been devised to determine whether an item is real property (goes with the land). For example, if curtains or draperies have been attached in such a way that they cannot be removed without damaging the home, they may be considered real property. But if they can easily be removed without damaging the home, they may be personal property. The purchase agreement should specify whether doubtful items are real or personal to avoid confusion later on.

Realtor®: A broker who is a member of the National Association of Realtors. Agents who are not members may not use the Realtor designation.

REO (Real Estate Owned): Property taken back through foreclosure and held for sale by a lender.

RESPA (Real Estate Settlement Procedures Act): Legislation requiring lenders to provide borrowers with specific information on the cost of securing financing. Basically it means that before you proceed far along the path of getting the mortgage, the lender has to provide you with an estimate of costs. Then, before you sign the documents binding you to the mortgage, the lender has to provide you with a breakdown of the actual costs.

Second Mortgage: An inferior mortgage usually placed on the property after a first mortgage. In the event of foreclosure, the second mortgage is paid off only if and when the first mortgage has been fully paid. Many lenders will not offer second mortgages.

Short Sale: Property sale in which a lender agrees to accept less than the mortgage amount in order to facilitate the sale and avoid a foreclosure.

SREA (Society of Real Estate Appraisers): A professional association to which qualified appraisers can belong.

Subject To: A contingency. Also a phrase often used to indicate that a buyer is not assuming the mortgage liability of a seller. For example, if the seller has an assumable loan and you (the buyer) assume the loan, you are taking over liability for payment. On the other hand, if you purchase subject to the mortgage, you do not assume liability for payment.

Subordination Clause: A clause in a mortgage document that keeps the mortgage subordinate to another mortgage.

Title: Legal evidence that you actually have the right of ownership of *Real Property*. It is given in the form of a deed (there are many different types of deeds) that specifies the kind of title you have (joint, common, or other).

Title Insurance Policy: An insurance policy that covers the title to a home. It may list the owner or the lender as beneficiary. The policy is issued by a title insurance company and specifies that if for any covered reason your title proves defective, the company will correct the title or compensate you up to a specified amount, usually the amount of the purchase price or the mortgage.

Trust Deed: A three-party lending arrangement that includes a borrower, or *trustor*; an independent third-party stakeholder, or *trustee* (usually a title insurance company); and a lender, or *beneficiary*, so-called because the lender stands to benefit if the trustee turns the deed over in case the borrower fails to make payments. The advantage of the trust deed over the mortgage is that foreclosure can be accomplished without court action. Usually there can be no deficiency judgment against the borrower. (In other words, if the property is worth less than the loan, the lender can't come back to the borrower after the sale for the difference.) See also *Purchase Money Mortgage.*

Upgrade: Any extra that a buyer may obtain when purchasing a new home—for example, a better-quality carpet or a wall mirror in the bedroom.

Upside Down: Owing more on a property than its market value.

VA Loan: A mortgage guaranteed by the U.S. Department of Veterans Affairs (VA). The VA actually guarantees only a small percentage of the loan amount, but since it guarantees the "top" of the monies loaned, lenders are willing to accept the arrangement. In a VA loan the government advances no money; rather, the mortgage is made by a private lender such as a bank.

Wraparound Financing: A blend of two mortgages, often used by sellers to get a higher interest rate or facilitate a sale. For example, instead of giving a buyer a simple *Second Mortgage*, the seller may combine the balance due on an existing mortgage (usually an existing first) with an additional loan. Thus the wrap includes both the second and the first mortgages. The borrower makes payments to the seller, who then keeps part of the payment and in turn pays off the existing mortgage.

Internet Resources

Robert Irwin, www.robertirwin.com   The author's Web site.

ESCROW–TITLE INSURANCE ORGANIZATIONS

ALTA form, www.alta.org/store/forms/homeown.pdf   Provides the basic form to comply with ALTA policies.

American Escrow Association, www.a-e-a.org   A major escrow trade association.

American Land Title Association, www.alta.org   A major trade association for professionals engaged in title research.

California Escrow Association, www.ceaescrow.org   California's trade association for professionals engaged in overseeing escrow accounts.

California Land Title Association, www.alta.org/store/forms/ homeown.pdf   California's trade association for professionals engaged in clearing titles.

Chicago Title Insurance Company, www.ctic.com   A major title insurance company.

First American Title Insurance Company, firstam.com   Major title insurance company.

Illinois Land Title Association, www.illinoislandtitle.org   The Illinois trade association for professionals handling title insurance.

Texas Land Title Association, www.tlta.com   The Texas trade association for title insurers.

GOVERNMENT AGENCIES

U.S. Department of Housing and Urban Development (HUD), www.hud.gov   Information on government programs including those involving settlement and/or closing procedures.

Federal Housing Administration (FHA), www.hud.gov/offices/ hsg/index.cfm   Information on FHA loan insurance and housing programs.

U.S. Department of Veterans Affairs (VA), www.va.gov   Information on VA loan guarantees and housing programs.

SECONDARY LENDERS

Fannie Mae, www.fanniemae.com and www.homepath.com   Loans, settlement procedures, and foreclosures.

Freddie Mac, www.freddiemac.com   Information on loans and settlement procedures.

Ginnie Mae, www.ginniemae.gov   Information on home purchasing and ownership.

CREDIT BUREAUS AND ORGANIZATIONS

Consumer Data Industry Associations, www.cdiaonline.org   Information on credit reports and credit laws.

Equifax, www.equifax.com   National credit reporting agency.

Experian, www.experian.com   National credit reporting agency.

Fair Isaac, www.fairisaac.com   Main credit scoring organization.

Federal Trade Commission, www.ftc.gov   Handles credit reporting complaints.

Trans Union, www.transunion.com   National credit reporting agency.

HOME INSPECTION ORGANIZATIONS

American Institute of Inspectors, www.inspection.org   A home inspection trade association.

American Society of Home Inspectors, www.ashi.com The most well known national home inspection trade association.

National Association of Certified Home Inspectors, www. nachi.org A national home inspection trade association.

OTHER RELATED ORGANIZATIONS

Dataquick, www.dataquick.com Provides information on real estate (fee).

National Association of Realtors, www.realtor.com Provides information on members, homes for sale, and other data.

Real Estate Settlement Providers Council, www.thelegaldescription.com Provides information and news on the laws affecting home closings.

The Legal Description, www.thelegaldescription.com Provides information and news on the laws affecting home closings.

Index

About the Author

Robert Irwin, one of America's leading experts in all areas of real estate, is the author of more than 50 books, including McGraw-Hill's best-selling Tips and Traps series and *Home Buyer's Checklist*. He has more than 30 years' experience as a real estate broker and has worked with agents, lenders, and consumers in helping to close home purchases. For more real estate tips and traps, go to www.robertirwin.com.